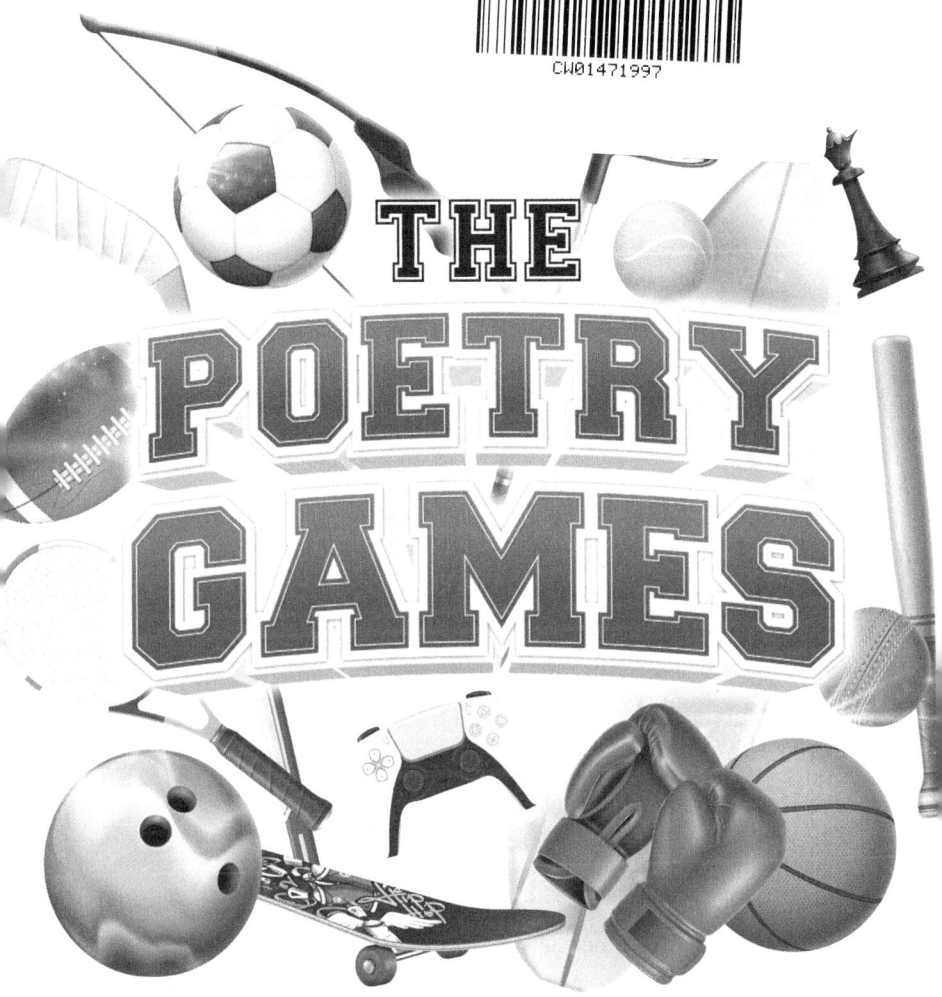

THE POETRY GAMES

GAME, SET, MATCH!

Edited By Byron Tobolik

First published in Great Britain in 2024 by:

Young Writers
Remus House
Coltsfoot Drive
Peterborough
PE2 9BF
Telephone: 01733 890066
Website: www.youngwriters.co.uk

All Rights Reserved
Book Design by Ashley Janson
© Copyright Contributors 2024
Softback ISBN 978-1-83685-040-3
Printed and bound in the UK by BookPrintingUK
Website: www.bookprintinguk.com
YB0619S

FOREWORD

Our latest competition, **THE POETRY GAMES**, focuses on games of all kinds. The summer of 2024 was packed with sport from the men's Euros to Wimbledon to the Olympics and more, providing loads of inspiration for aspiring writers. They've written about their sporting heroes, their own sporting aspirations or a sport they enjoy. We also asked them to consider other games and pastimes, so they didn't have to be restricted to sport! Video games, board games, card games, playground games… anything that brings them fun!

Here at Young Writers our aim is to encourage creativity in children and to inspire a love of the written word, so it's great to get such an amazing response, with some absolutely fantastic poems. The result is a collection of poems in a variety of poetic styles that also showcase their creativity and writing ability. Seeing their work in print will encourage them to keep writing as they grow and become our poets of tomorrow.

I'd like to congratulate all the young poets in this anthology, it's a wonderful achievement and I hope this inspires you to continue with your creative writing.

CONTENTS

Kalen Noel (10)	114	Ryan King (15)	157
Charlie Wallace (7)	115	Hafsa Nasir Choudhry (10)	158
Patrycja Michalska (11)	116	Matthew Heeks (13)	159
Jacob Burton (10)	117	Nia Roberts (10)	160
Hafsa Muhammad Nusair (13)	118	Kartik Kamble (9)	161
Kenechi Ezeajughi (16)	119	James Edwards (12)	162
Lana Al-Taie (13)	120	Noah Murton (10)	163
Aurelia Littlejohn (16)	121	Ibukun Durojaiye (13)	164
Muhammad Umar (11)	122	Bridget Frimpong (17)	165
Emmie Hayward (14)	123	Hazel Foster (10)	166
Ayat Waseem Khan (9)	124	Olivia Dodimead (9)	167
Christina Lucille Young (4)	125	Ryley Patterson (12)	168
Sumera Arshad (14)	126	Ambar Javed (10)	169
Eliza Ray (13)	127	Evelyn Hardy (12)	170
Chloe Willcox (14)	128	Larissa Gray (12)	171
Benjamin Doeteh (18)	129	Athmika Jeyakanth (10)	172
Caitlan Bridge (14)	130	Emily Garrett (10)	173
Asana Draman (8)	131	Logan James Jones (9)	174
Sharon Saini (15)	132	Gracie Peach (10)	175
Amelia Barnes (13)	133	Lily Bayliff (10)	176
Deborah Adesanya (14)	134	Katherine Clough (14)	177
Cody Garrett (9)	135	Teiarnie Moore (10)	178
Aaditri Manjunath (11)	136	Victoria Cicha (16)	179
Khadija Aktar (11)	137	Lilly Woosnam-Jones (10)	180
Raeesah Khan (11)	138	Lenny Wyatt (10)	181
Ayana Khan (11)	139	Emily Howitt (7)	182
Chizzy Unachukwu (10)	140	Amber Sedighi (11)	183
Emiline Anderson-Kalsi (11)	141	Philippa Julian (10)	184
Isla Eves-Davis (9)	142	Isla Longden (10)	185
Toby West (6)	143	Ava Clark (12)	186
Evie Ansell-Rodgers (16)	144	Ava Knighton (8)	187
Zoe Worth (12)	145	Harry Pearson (6)	188
Ahana Madhok (10)	146	Harrison Farmer (9)	189
Fareedah Adenusi (10)	147	Jennifer Jenkins (12)	190
Sky Lawton (17)	148	Suhani Das (13)	191
Gracie Chapman (14)	149	Hope Miles (9)	192
Shreekant Baravkar (10)	150	Syeda Anisa Mumtaz Nakvi (11)	193
Ananya Sanil Balakrishnan (12)	151	Arianna Fordyce (7)	194
Eilidh Graham (10)	152	Oaklee Dando (5)	195
Joshua Otalor (5)	153	Ayra Jamal (9)	196
Raihan Farooq (13)	154	Beatrice Elizabeth Matiukhina (9)	197
Elsie Rich (10)	155	Joshua Brown (13)	198
Lily Wall (12)	156	Pareeza Umar (12)	199

Sukhman Kaur (8)	200
Elika Rafiee (9)	201
Edie Cook (14)	202
Florence Reed (11)	203
Esha Raheel (10)	204
Caydon Reed (12)	205
Imogen Lewis (7)	206
Bencharis Nso (11)	207
Dominykas Dapkevicius (10)	208
Sahejveer Kaur Sheri (7)	209
Sahil Agrawal (10)	210
Hailie Valletta (4)	211
Fatima Ceesay (9)	212
Zachary Flounders (9)	213
Faith Kelly (15)	214
Jackson Peach (7)	215
Caden Hamlyn-Harris (11)	216
Momin Suleman (13)	217
Eilidh Ortega (10)	218
Anna Heathcote (7)	219
Lilly Wallace (5)	220
Kat McCue (8)	221
Liv Kennedy (9)	222
Còiseam Young	223
Ewan Jones (17)	224
Amirah Bekhit (9)	225
Jessica Prestage (12)	226
Taylor-Grace Stare (10)	227
Taylor Powell (9)	228
Zakariya Hersi (9)	229
Bonnie Taylor (9)	230
Pippa Ward (7)	231
Miles Lewis (5)	232
Elizabeth Byrom (9)	233
Vaanathi Manikandan (11)	234
Thananiya Thevakanthan (9)	235
Brendan Cosgrove (10)	236

Ansford Academy, Castle Cary

Elsie Honnor (13)	237

Ark Blake Academy, Croydon

Lia Chung (13)	238

Brixham College, Brixham

Eve Antroness	239

Bruern Abbey Senior School, Chilton

Charlie Thomas (15)	240

Devonport High School For Girls, Peverell

Nafisa Chowdhury (13)	241

Friern Barnet School, Friern Barnet

Karim Rodrick (12)	243

Goddard Park Primary School, Park North

Omari Bramble	244
Millie May Saunders (9)	245
Riley Hobbs (9)	246
Alfie Pockett (8)	247
Lola Hamley	248
Rayyan Musid (9)	249
Phoebe Banham (9)	250
Elisha Comrie	251
Genesis Rai (9)	252
Christie Do Rosario	253
Archie Haines (10)	254
Jack Saunders (9)	255
Faith J (9)	256
Esmai Tina Fanning (9)	257
Alex Lourenco	258
Alfie W (9)	259

Running Deer School CIC, Butterdon Wood

Torridon Primary School, Catford

Unity Academy, Blackpool

THE
POEMS

The Great Tesco Pie Overload Explained

I chewed my pencil. What to write?
When my teacher told me to make up a sport,
I thought I would be quick. How wrong was I?
Ideas? Ideas? I can't think of a thing.
A ball game? A fall game? Wait... I've got a game!
A game where you have to take flight,
And the only way to pass the tiny ball is to flick!
And you have to flick the ball into the hoop very high,
But blocking your way is a piece of floating string,
So, to score a point, you must have very good aim!

And you fly on what? Well, it might bite,
But I think a scaled squid with sharp teeth is the best thing
to pick!
The team with the most points wins; the losers turn into pie!
Then the winners eat them up; so a napkin, you better bring,
Because when you're a mess, you'll be the one to blame!
I handed my homework to my teacher who was quite polite,
He said he was thinking of a sport where the losers don't
get licked, but the class disagreed!
They voted for mine to win the prize:
Turning your sport into a real thing!

So that's why there are so many pies in Tesco at the
moment. You're welcome.

Daisy Stockford (11)

1

Echoes In The Feed

In the long night's embrace, we seek the light,
In this endless shade, we search for sight.
The emptiness we carry, the burdens we bear,
A sea to wade, a climb to dare.
Let the singular sphere echo this song,
That even as we fell, we rose strong.
That even in darkness, we shone bright,
That even in loss, we found the fight.
Dear hearts, united here today,
Bound by threads the modern age displays,
Social media, once a beacon's light,
Now casts shadows in the night.
Our hearts ache for true connection,
In this false glow of digital affection.
A river, at first, gentle in its sweep,
Now a torrent, eroding deep.
A road that seemed flat begins to rise,
A hill that grows steep before our eyes.
We climb to reach the real world's side,
Before this hill becomes too high.
Questions arise about indulgence in virtual realms,
In Snapchat's tales or Facebook's helms.
If the answer is no, they look with disbelief,
Curiosity follows, then dismissive grief.

They call it boring, for refusal
Of the virtual mask others choose.
But that world is rich with reality's hue,
While theirs is filtered, theirs is true.
Smiles are seen unframed by screens,
Laughter is heard purely, not in digital scenes.
The aroma of love's own feast is smelt,
Moments that cannot cease are tasted.
They hide behind their glowing walls,
In a world that traps and calls.
Life is lived in reality's warm embrace,
Feeling textures, life's true face.
Whose fault is this? All must ponder,
As we let social media pull under.
It promises connection, delivers isolation,
A siren's song, a desolation.
Parents, remember when first it was bought
That game, that phone, the future sought.
A portal was opened, unknowing, unaware,
To a world where connection is rare.
Screens were given, yet wonder why
Eyes do not look eye to eye.
Allowed escape, then question
Solitude and depression.
Family - Father and Mother, I love you,
A circle of strength, a bond true.

In simple moments, true connection thrives,
Beyond the screens, real life survives.
Why do we let social media divide,
Control our lives, where genuine moments hide?
Why replace real with the artificial,
Let it rule, make the superficial official?
Everywhere, young eyes strained,
From screens their beauty drained.
Anxiety, stress, depression rise,
Invisible chains in a digital guise.
If we continue, we see a decline,
In humans, in humanity, a chilling sign.
Frozen bodies in every mirror,
A dystopian nightmare growing nearer.
Break these chains, let freedom ring,
Unplug from the digital string.
Listen to nature's soft sighs,
See the world through clear eyes.
Hear the ocean's calming waves,
Find the peace your spirit craves.
Return to the heart of our soul,
To what makes us truly whole.

Sara Mohammad (14)

Money

Money, that's what the Monopoly Man needed.
Maybe money was the way, maybe that's how he succeeded.
Maybe Old Kent Road or a plan to get The Strand.
He ran and ran with a chest in his hand.
Full with bags of his merry load.
Maybe he could buy a house on Whitechapel Road.
Win a beauty contest or advance to Go.
Monopoly Man was getting desperate now,
So he robbed and robbed till his house fell down.
He was caught, actually caught, with his treasures and troves,
Weighed down by fees and lost all his roads.
Thrown in jail was the old man's life,
He had to roll a six to see the light.
Then, by chance, he was sent a card - 'Get Out of Jail Free'!
He jumped out of prison and smiled with glee.
So off to Park Lane, not by boat, but by train.
As he travelled and travelled, his future unravelled.
The Monopoly Man then realised money was not what he needed.
He had love and a family, he had already succeeded.
His wife was Mayfair and children were Park Lane,
As he twiddled his moustache and knew he wouldn't be the same.

Elsie Lymer (10)

Just GOAT Things

One peaked in the Catalan county, the other at majestic Madrid,
Cristiano Ronaldo and Lionel Messi, two magical, manic madmen,
The best football players to ever live.
As much as it hurts to say, their era is quickly coming to an end,
Messi the Catalan king and Ronaldo the European emperor.
Let's talk about maestro Messi,
Went to Barcelona at a young age,
Something he was remembered for.
After a few years at La Masia, his impact was heavy,
Formed a duo with Ronaldinho the wizard,
Won the Champions League four times and the Ballon d'Or eight.
But in 2012, he did one of the craziest things I've ever heard,
This psycho scored ninety-one goals in all competitions,
Not letting goalkeepers take a break.
And his partnership with Suarez and Neymar wasn't even fair.
In 2015, Neymar scored 30, my bad, 48 goals in all competitions,
But Messi was like: "We're not playing games here."
And this man scored 52; he went on a quest of chaos and destruction,
And won the Ballon d'Or again, no surprises there.

And in the 2022 World Cup, he was on fire,
He was everyone's biggest nightmare.
If anyone says different, they are a liar.
Now, he's balling out in the United States.

Now, let's talk about King Cristiano,
People think his fans have the wildest takes,
That's fair but you can't hate on Ronaldo.
From Madeira to Lisbon, then to Manchester, Madrid, Turin,
Manchester and now Riyadh,
Balling out, decimating teams here and there.
Can we just sit and marvel at what an illustrious career he had.
Champions League, league titles, Ballon d'Ors and golden boots everywhere,
And he's been doing it for more than 20 years.
Cristiano in 2008 was scary, finding the net 42 times.
He won all that there was to win individually that year.
Being that good has to be a punishable crime,
And noodle-haired Ronaldo was even more unfair.
He made legendary teams wet their pants.
In 2018, against Juventus, Cristiano leapt into the air,
Scored a beautiful bicycle kick that even got Juventus chants,
Made Zidane think his hair grew back.
So good, Juventus signed him for a mouth-watering sum.
There was nothing this monster lacked,
These two made watching the La Liga fun,

Hail Lionel Messi and Cristiano Ronaldo,
And thank you for everything.

Adriel Willoughby (13)

Basketball At The Olympics

B asketball is the best
A bove the opponent's head, the basketball goes
S ome people in basketball do slam dunks
K ids even like to watch basketball
E ven women can play
T he hoops have been designed nicely
B asketball is fun
A ir goes onto the player's face when they jump
L abels on the back of vests show their names
L ay-ups are a wonderful shot

A dults play basketball
T hey wear vests so that they don't sweat

T heir passes are slick
H oops are really cool
E xtra time in basketball is good for the basketball players

O nce the whistle is blown, the game has ended
L ive basketball means that it is happening right now
Y ellow basketballs are amazing
M aximum time is 48 minutes
P arks often have basketball courts
I t has a marvellous court
C urved shots are shots that are looped
S crews attach the hoop to the pole.

Samuel Kiwanuka-Musoke (7)

My City

An indescribable word
A word that describes culture
A word that describes childhood
A word that describes fame
A word that can have so many meanings
Yet be understood in actions presented in games

When I think of it, I think of my culture
My face painted in the flag of England
When watching the football
Flags dotted round the house
Proclaiming myself as their number one fan
Even though I can't kick a ball
Watching the TV in awe
Shooting up when someone shoots and scores
Singing the country's anthem,
Even if we didn't win the World Cup
That's the one true meaning of sport
The indescribable word
That can have so many meanings
Yet be understood in actions presented in games.

When I think of it, I also think of my childhood
The sports I played that shaped me into who I am today
The sports that brought me closer to my friends
My family, my pets

The sports that I competed in to win medals
The sports that raised money for charity
Like running 5K
Or reading as many books as I could in a day
That's the other true meaning of sport
The memories you hold
Using it to help others who can't play sport
The indescribable word
That can have so many meanings
Yet be understood in actions presented in games.

When I think of it, I finally think of fame
The Olympics I watched since I was little
Cheering them on as they were my idols
From when runners swept the track clean
High jumpers swiftly gliding through the air
Swimmers swimming like fish through the water
I wanted to be just like them
Famous like them
People watching me like I watched them
That's the final true meaning of sport
Wanting fame to inspire others not for greed
Just to be watched for your hobby in sport
The indescribable word
That can have so many meanings
Yet be portrayed in actions presented in games.

Robyn Watmough (15)

United!

Five famous rings bring people together,
These games have been going on practically forever.
All started with some simple sprinting and running,
Since then, every year it keeps on coming.

Proud people stand representing their home,
Want to receive a medal and really get known.
The flame, their eyes and passion it is lighting,
Because to get to the top, they will be fighting.

Everyone is diving into the Olympic Games,
Watching all these well-known names.
Cheering for who they love and believe in,
Knowing in their eyes, they already own a win.

America is next but Paris is now and fresh,
Hoping to put other hosts and games to the test.
New sports are coming every year, weird and wacky,
Modern and not ancient, new and not tacky.

You cannot take your eyes off a single race,
In case you miss who is in first place.
Everyone is watching for over two weeks straight,
Looking so intently, that for work, they are late.

But then it is the end and you have to say goodbye,
We shall all meet again the very next time.

You can all take your kit off and take a deep breath,
Get some long sleep and very well-earned rest.

But wait, you have got the Paralympics next, hooray,
All of this again, you can unpause and replay.
More unforgettable competition is arriving,
With some more young athletes who are thriving.

Working much harder than anybody else,
Getting up instead of feeling sorry for themselves.
Achieving what nobody thought they were capable of,
Showing to everyone their true strength and love.

Put your running shoes back on and get ready to race,
Now there is more and more you need to pick up the pace.
So much to choose from, I do not know how you can decide,
Through everything, you should take a light, long stride.

Luna Stevens (11)

Back In Time To The Land Of Chariots

I think I would like to go back in time, to the land of ultimate influence,
Where the blazing sun lay in the sapphire sky and scorched the city below,
From Milon of Croton to Leonidas of Rhodes; famous even after their time,
Painted in everlasting bronze and fading memories.
Yes, I would like to go there.

Not for that though, rather I would like to go to see the Circus Maximus,
A circular stone giant, the home of gladiators,
battles and glory,
Where the motto is to 'fight or be fought... to death'.
Where great tales are shared over generations and generations... and a generation more.

Chariot racing. An action-packed sport for a rip-roaring life,
It came with yelling, pushing, shoving and, of course, the risk of sleeping... well, forever.
Despite this, I would still like to go!
People at the time spoke of wondrous, enthralling moments bound to be etched in one's mind
Till even Gaia herself couldn't make the rock tremble at her commands.

Imagine! The cool wind blowing past your silky locks while you and your partner attempt to steel your nerves for this afternoon's tournament.
It's no use though, you're not a champion like Diocles and you're most certainly not a Flavius Scorpus,
And because it's summer in the Hellas, there is no cool wind blowing past you, just everyday hot and dry weather.
The usual summer deal.

If you asked me the question: 'What is your favourite sport?'
My answer would never change; my favourite sport is extinct and dried up never to be the same,
Driven by wild creatures created by the sea,
My chariot from Greece is what I would go and see,
If only I could go back and time travel to be there again.

A celebration of the world of games,
A celebration of past and present events.
Cheers to... Chariot racing.

Glory Daramola (16)

Risk

Once, twice over the board
Hesitate, shuffle, reorganise
Turn left or right or attack from the back
Tides of plastic armies at your bidding, under your hand
Under your personal command, easily viewed and easily moved
Predictable and always controlled - they will not resist you
Symbolic figures; it doesn't matter if they are defeated
Back in the box, at the side, so what?
It's the risk, but you have more
To take their place
They can't complain

Once, twice over the board
Send armies in or out
Not personally, but you need only ask others to do so...
And they will. The power trickles down to each wielder
Though you're in charge - or are you?
Everything is simplified
Little toys on a board
A child's game of fighting
Distant and not real - you're not there!
The detached strategist
Who needs to see from above and small
To do their job

Yet here's the truth:

Your army toys are unpredictable
Out of your sight and not so easily decamped
Not always - or just not - controlled by you
You and your tiered, distancing, necessary hierarchy of power
Real life is never as simple as a board and its pieces
And whom do you risk?
You risk no cold, tiny, plastic figures
The lives defeated are not mere unfeeling ones
You cannot just set them aside casually and think, *oh, it's all right*
For you command a tide
Of flesh and blood and spirit
Of real people, who feel and live
Their fates are real
The battles are real
(But not to you)
You can't control them like plastic soldiers
They can't complain - not to you directly
You, the player of this game
The one at the faraway flatness of the symbolic board
But this is no game -

This is a war.

Anna Wong (16)

I Just Won Sports Day!

It was real.
How did I feel?
Amazed and dazed,
In a victory haze.

I just won Sports Day!
At the age of ten.
Felt good in every way,
How did I do that then?

I got a first
In an 800m run,
I was dying of thirst
And felt so glad I was done.

Another first place,
In a 400m run,
It was a tough race,
But also kind of fun.

A 60m sprint, I won,
And yes! I got a first
Felt so proud of what I'd done,
With happiness, I could have burst.

I just won Sports Day!
At the age of ten.

Felt good in every way,
What else did I do then?

I also got a first
In the egg and spoon race.
It really was too funny,
You should have seen my face!

A first in hurdles,
Leap! Leap! Leap!
At the finish line,
I fell down in a heap.

First in speed bounce,
Side to side of a cone.
61 bounces in under a minute,
A quick, rhythmic drone.

I got a first in long jump,
I jumped rather far.
Then me and my friend,
We joyfully began to spar.

I just won Sports Day,
At the age of ten.
Proud in every way,
What were my other medals then?

Oh and in high jump,
I happily won a second.

Earned that prize in triumph,
Jumped higher than I reckoned.

About my thirds,
I'll share just one.
In javelin, a surprise,
But still, it was fun.

Competitions, there were more.
At worst, I placed 4th.
In total, there were 11,
Out of these, I won in 7.

Seven firsts,
Out of eleven.
Felt like stepping,
Into heaven.

I just won Sports Day,
Shouting out, "Woohoo!"
Had a really great time,
Let's hope you do too.

Ananya Jindal (10)

England's England-Like Euros Run

England finished the group with two draws and a win,
Southgate put Trent in midfield, that was his pick,
Then came Jude Bellingham's last-minute overhead kick.
In the semi-finals was the flawless penalty shootout,
Against the Netherlands in the 90th minute,
Watkins scored to make it two-one,
Which meant we made the finals.
We had to face a Spain team,
With Lamine Yamal and Nico Williams,
Who beat both Germany and France,
With the same scoreline of two-one.
Now everything is said and done,
I think we could have won.
After a goal from Spain's Nico and
England's Cole Palmer,
Where the finish was definitely cold!
But it wasn't enough as they scored another goal,
Centimetres from offside.
Sadly, then we heard the final whistle,
That made the England fans cry.
After this, people always say there's always next time,
But I think:
Can we please win the Euros
for the first time in our history!

John Adams (9)

My Game

If I could make a sport, it would be brought
To a stadium, where if they dared
Decide to play, they would have to stay,
Even if it'd been two days,
If they did, I'd ensure everyone knew,
That you would never be seen again.

"How do you play the game?" you might ask.
Well, it's a very, very simple task.
As soon as you step across the line,
That shows that you're officially mine.
To play, you must say what abilities you have,
So I can decide whether I want you to go through.

The goal of the game is really simple,
Easier than popping a pimple.
There's a book in the middle of the stage
And you must get it first and read every page.

The skills you need might be easy for you, indeed,
But if you struggle to read, then this isn't your cup of tea.

What do you win?
Ahh, well, you see, you get to keep the book.
Isn't that wonderful?
Well, so you don't think I'm dull,
There is one last thing that you might need,

An unlimited pass to have for free,
Every book you want to read.

And if you want to be a writer,
We've got the right starter.
You get an editor and a publisher all in one go.
So if that's what you dream,
You would beg so much,
You would kick and scream.

Then come down tomorrow,
As we are going to put a stop to your sorrow.
The game is Wednesday,
I hope to see you there.
And I do care and hope you come.
If you want to compete, then be afraid,
We have lots of cheaters, but it's okay,
For the pit of doom is where they will get sent away.

So in your free time,
Come and have the best time.
At the spine-chilling,
Most terrifying game *ever!*

Darcie O'Toole (11)

The Beautiful Game

The WSL kicked off with a bang,
Fans chanting like a massive gang.
Players were riled up, thinking, *this is the moment*,
The aim of the game: beat the opponent.
Fans, in their thousands, sat in suspense,
The beautiful game, this feeling is immense.
Players look around, loving what they're seeing.
The Euros kicked this off, this is only the beginning!

Goals, goals in the net,
Celebrating like it's the best.

Three points are all they want,
Teams picking up, this is getting hot.
But with Earps, Hampton, and Keating in goal,
The WSL teams could easily fold.
Superstars shining through,
James, Hemp, Russo, and Toone,
Too many more to say,
But wow, it's exciting to watch them play.

Goals, goals in the net,
Celebrating like it's the best.

There's been some suffering, they suffer for their art.
Roebuck, Maanum & ACLs for a start.

The ACL epidemic is in full stride,
But ups and downs are part of the ride.
High stake games, everyone's in it to win it,
Beth Mead returns, two goals in two minutes.

Goals, goals in the net,
Celebrating like it's the best.

Arsenal beat Chelsea 4-1, no sun!
But whatever the weather, the Gunners stuck it to Emma.
From the bottom to the top, these girls wear their badge with pride,
All of the fans along for the ride.

Goals, goals in the net,
Celebrating like it's the best.

Though she is but little, she is fierce,
It's taken so long for them to see us.
Now, records are breaking one by one,
Smashing stereotypes 'til they're gone!

Codie-Leigh Copping (16)

Chess Challenge

Of all games, there's one that requires the most thought
Defending, attacking the board where you fought
It took me an extremely long time to master
Because chess is a game where you can't think faster

First are the pawns - the toy foot soldiers
Promotion is the weight on their advancing shoulders
As I begin the game, ready to do battle
I know I must step up to the mantle

Knights have the advantage, they move in an unusual way
Jumping over pieces to get in and out of the play
I must be clever and use them to their best
For they can take many pieces and be a real pest

Bishops cross the board diagonally, taking a stand
And can often be very useful to have at hand
I have to be careful and use them most wisely
They can be lethal and brutal if used timely

Rooks are brilliant and can be quite devastating
Moving horizontally and vertically, most aggravating
If played correctly to join in the attack
For my opponent, there may be no coming back

The queen is a most formidable foe
Who causes the enemy much worry and woe

She is also precious as one mistake can cost
You do not want the most powerful piece to be lost

The king is a rather curious matter
If I checkmate him, your game is shattered
Yet he can only move one square at a time
To get out of check is often hard to find

I have to be on alert with no distractions
To make sure all my moves are good reactions
It has taken me years and oh how I have tried
But finally beating Dad has filled me with pride!

Shaye Gregory (12)

My Euros Dream

The fans will never stop,
Some matches, they will hop.
We're trophy cold, Kane's getting old,
Our chances have been blocked.
But in Southgate's locker,
There are secrets about soccer,
To stop us flying home again in an empty chopper.
Goodbye to losing all,
And feeling very small.
Just get over the line,
And it will leave you feeling fine.

Well, there's football,
And there's football,
After every game, we will inch closer,
Come on lads, let's put it together,
We'll win, whatever the weather.
Football will come home.

Have you watched the last game?
No.
Oh, you haven't lived at all.
Just go on channel one or three,
And you'll be as happy as a bee.

Is the formation feeling bad?
Is it making you feel sad?

Don't worry, at least Kane's up front,
Will that make you glad?
It makes us feel frustration,
Like when you've got constipation,
Trent whacks it in the corner,
Without a hint of hesitation.

Well, there's football,
And there's football,
After every game, we will inch closer,
Come on lads, let's put it together,
We might be winners forever.
Football might come home.

Well, there are winners and there are losers,
When you're watching with your mates in the local boozer.
Come on lads, let's put it together.
Football might come home,
After all of the tournaments we roamed.
One of them, we'll own.
Maybe we'll have to wait till it's in Rome.

Ellie Sheppard (12)

Fencing: Attack And Parry!

This is it,
The finals of the Youth Championships,
The one-minute break,
My clubmates swarm towards me,
"You've got this!" yells one,
"Yeah, you can do it!" yells another,
Blood pulsates in my ears,
It's impossible to hear their cheers,
But I hear one,
Not a cheer,
"Attack in preparation, he goes slow at the start to see if he
should chase."
My coach breaks through my tired trance,
I joined this club three years ago,
Looking to find my place in sport,
And I found it,
I can't let that go to waste!
I must win,
The break is over,
The score is four-all,
I prepare myself in the on guard,
My opponent looking at me,
Ready to attack and parry,
My mind fills with worry,
Can I do it or can I not?

There is no time to ponder,
"En garde, prêt, allez."
I take in a rapid breath,
And I step with unexpected swiftness.
I plunge my right leg forward into the sharp, metal piste,
My arm instinctively thrusting forward towards his head,
A perfect lunge,
So hasty, he couldn't have reacted,
Right?
"We have a winner of the... youth championships!"
Cheers once again flood my brain,
I feel my friends run up to me from behind and hug me,
Turning our club into what is better described as a mob,
I feel so dizzy,
Like I'm about to fall,
My legs shake beneath my weight and my chest might explode,
But I did it,
I grin,
I won.

Emma Mareva (14)

Cowboys Like Us

In the world of bull riding,
Where courage meets the beast,
We face a daring challenge,
A remarkable feat.

The arena's musty air,
Swooning the rider's jaw,
The spectators blare,
Drunk on the crowd's uproar.

The adrenaline rush,
To the danger faced,
We take our stand,
Against a daring brand.

The bulls' bodies bucking,
And their snouts steaming,
Their spirit cannot be tamed,
But cowboys like us seek a change.

Each eight-second ride,
No room for mistakes,
Is the price of a drill,
Worth a few moments of thrill?

In the hush of moments lost,
Whispers of change softly caress my soul,

Questions unasked, thoughts unspoken,
A silent symphony takes its toll.

Motivation's plea, a distant scream,
Urging me to defy the shadows cast,
Yet indifference lingers, a bittersweet refrain,
Of a past that couldn't last.

Battered, bruised, like thatch worn thin,
My body is a testament to time's cruel jest,
In need of repair, yet some wounds run too deep,
A lifetime of trials put to the test.

To quit is to surrender, to concede defeat,
A victory handed to those who doubt,
Yet the thrill of risk has lost its charm,
The fire that once burned now flickers out.

A life once vibrant, ablaze with youth's fervour,
Now a quieter, tempered flame,
The echoes of 24, a distant memory,
Of a time that will never be the same.

Violet Miller (18)

Whispers Of The Water

In deep waters where silence reigns,
A swimmer moves, free from chains,
With every stroke, a dance so light,
In liquid realms, they take their flight.

The sun above shines a golden hue,
Reflecting on waves, a sparkling view,
Beneath the surface, calm and clear,
A world of wonder is drawing near.

With arms outstretched, they cut the tide,
In rhythmic grace, they smoothly glide,
Each breath a whisper, soft and slow,
In tranquil depths, they ebb and flow.

The water cool, a gentle embrace,
A soothing balm, a tender grace,
It cradles them in buoyant arms,
Away from life's relentless harm.

In freestyle's rush, they find their speed,
In backstroke's ease, they take the lead,
With butterfly's strength, they soar and dive,
In breaststroke's calm, they feel alive.

The pool, a canvas, blue and wide,
Where dreams and goals are magnified,

Each lap a journey, each turn a quest,
In the heart of water, they find their best.

The crowd may cheer, the lights may gleam,
But in the water, they chase a dream,
A solitary path, yet not alone,
In every splash, their spirit's shown.

For swimming is a timeless art,
A blend of body, mind and heart,
In every stroke, a story told,
Of courage, strength and spirits bold.

So let them swim in joy and grace,
In whimsical waters, their sacred space,
For in the depths, they find their song,
A melody that carries on.

Anabella Calfa (13)

The Badminton Mishap

It was Zoe's competition day,
She waved her parents goodbye,
And she was soon on her way.
Stressed, she was feeling,
As she stared at the coach's ceiling.
She soon arrived, feeling a fright,
It's going to be alright,
She said to herself.
All she wanted to do
Was make her parents proud.
It was her time,
Soon, she would shine.
She picked up her badminton rac',
The other contestant's name was Jack.
"I've got this," she muttered,
The sound of the racquets clattered together.
The loud whistle blew,
The sight of shuttlecocks flew.
She missed and she tripped,
It was unfortunately the end of the round.
Jack scored one, Zoe scored zero.
Zoe felt hopeless,
But she didn't let this get her down,
She joined the second round,
The whistle blew again.

In the crowd, she saw her friend,
This gave her hope and she was off again.
It was getting close to a tie,
But Jack missed,
Zoe scored one.
The whistle blew again.
Game faces on.
Everyone's breath was held,
Zoe hit the shuttlecock,
And Jack missed.
"Hooray!" everyone cheered,
Zoe's parents appeared.
They came to surprise her,
It felt like a blur.
She went to go collect her medal,
Her journey was stressful.
But she had done it -
Once again.

Jennifer Howarth (16)

The Cheetah Will Always Beat A Lion

The cheetah will always beat a lion.
Take your marks,
All goes quiet, your mind slows.
Don't focus on rivals or crowds,
Or how loud their whistles the wind blows.

The cheetah shakes his back leg to taunt the audience, so they screech louder than brakes.
He rolls in it, the attention and praise, the love he gets for being the best, no matter how much effort it takes.
But I keep my head down and breathe.
No one is cheering for me when their winner is already guaranteed.
I'm aware of my hind legs, my back and my shoulders,
I don't think about the crowd or their screams,
I need to feed.

"Ready, set..."
He smirks smugly at me.
But my mind and head space can't be touched,
He doesn't know it, he wouldn't believe it.
In his head, he's already won,
That makes him weak.
My mind is closed off from everything,
Except for the starting gun.

I know I'm ready,
After all the sweat in my eyes, my teeth, my body and my
feet begin to leak.
Bang!
Nothing but the track.
And then you feel it. Your heart. *Thump.*
Back into your chest.
Your brain going at a thousand miles per hour,
And my breath comes back.
In history, in the world and in the universe.
All because of mentality.
'The cheetah will always beat a lion' was reversed.

Amber Mclaren (14)

Tennis And My Ma

I'mma go out there and season my serve,
Watch that ball cook with a single curve,
Slicin' and dicin' till I get what I deserve
He knows I'm devouring, with my swagger and style
Why'd you think they call me the une bête de tennis?
Cos my reflexes be wild.
The court is shaking,
Cos I'm breathtaking, as I take
That breath away.
He knows that he's lost,
Knows that I've won,
Cos that ball is my man,
And on the penultimate serve,
My bro is done.

Jesse D. Elrod
Is who I am,
Watched King Richard with my momma so many times,
I'm all open stance till I dance like a flame.

"Why you so petty?" my momma will always say.
"You're just being mad, cos my racket puts you at bay."
You sigh, cos life's harder when your ma says she's here to
rally and slay.
And yo' ma puts her hands on her hips,
Pouts her lips,
"And that attitude got Serena Williams nowhere, Jesse."

My ma's pure black, dreads the colour of her racket,
Wears all 60s, with her '62 California jacket.
But, you're all smooth, you groundstroke like The Karate Kid,
Your ma has to groan when your d-d-d-drop shots are fluid.

But I know I'm cooked, when Ma
Says to train, or else
At dinner, she'll eat the plantain.

Zack Kiraga (13)

My Student PE Teacher

Once I had a teacher,
Proud as can be,
Every day, he polished his trophies,
Come to my school and I swear you'll see!

He teaches everything
Swimming, skiing, football, basketball,
He even runs Sports Day,
And that's not all,

Jumping, running, sprinting, catching,
The list goes on,
Skipping, tennis, rounders, baseball,
If you think there's more, you're not wrong,

There was a time,
Mr Physical was stumped,
When he got beaten by a girl,
And ran off in a grump!

It was a skipping race,
Mr Physical's specialty,
A little girl of about five came,
Then, to himself, he smiled smugly,

"There's no way you can beat me!"
He then made a face like a troll,

He kept taunting the girl,
'Til he got tired of the mean role,

"Okay, race starting in 1, 2, 3,"
Said my friend, Jeremy, eager to see the fight,
Mr Physical got off to a slow start,
But this little girl practically took flight!

She did the loop-de-loop,
The backwards skip,
Even though all this happened,
The PE teacher couldn't go quick!

He got tired halfway,
And blamed arthritis,
But usually only people above 30 get it,
So really, no excuses, Ed Physical is just obnoxious!

Estrela Loutsaris (10)

An Ode To Chess

The pieces stand tall, the pieces stand high,
Standing on their battlefield,
Marching along, bravely fighting,
Until their opponent yields.

The brave pawn, the backbone of chess,
Supports his soldier friends,
Moving one square at a time, they together make a wall,
Though he may be small, he can defend.

The armoured knight jumps into enemy land,
With the force of unpredictability,
Before you know it, he's destroyed your position,
And he's making your king flee.

The bishop, the sniper of the group,
Hiding, he lies in wait,
And unnoticed, he captures the opponent's queen,
The game is over, on your side comes fate.

The rook, the fortified tower of strength,
He castles with the king,
And he stares at the centre, nothing is safe,
He finally checkmates, declaring his win.

The queen, the most powerful of the ranks,
She captures every piece,

Nothing on the board could ever stop her,
She attacks without mercy or peace.

The king, the leader and strategy-maker,
He hides himself away,
And brings his pieces into battle,
The opponent's king shall pay.

The pieces stand tall, the pieces stand high,
Exchanges, traps and pins,
The battle of wits continues,
Until one or the other wins.

Rajesh Raha (10)

Morals Of Fighting

Respect is giving a bow,
To black belts and senseis who show you how.
It's being prepared and ready without being asked,
And giving it 100% in every class.

Fairness is sticking to the book,
Blitz, back fist or spinning hook.
Bowing shows you're ready for the test,
Just don't go thinking you're better than the rest.

Determination is the true martial art,
The potential to finish what you start.
It's refusing to give up when things get tough,
Or starting to cry when sparring gets rough.
It's not giving up when your muscles start to shake,
No matter how many tries it takes.

Discipline is the ability to focus,
When it goes wrong, you can notice.
It's taking a breath when things make you mad,
Then walking away because fighting is bad.
As every sensei says: 'Fighting stays in the dojo."
Stick to this until shown so.

Good spirit is portraying no fear,
Or running away when trouble is near.

It's knowing on your journey, that there are some
risks you must take,
And along the way, some mistakes you might make.
It's standing up proudly, no matter what happens,
And not being predictable by mixing your patterns.

Imogen Nathan (16)

Jumanji: The Game That Plays You

Holed up and hidden in an empty attic,
Lays a treacherous board game, still as static.
Tucked in for dozens of centuries,
Rotting for life with nostalgic memories.

A boy named Alex, curious and keen,
Wanted to unleash the game that lay unseen.
The drum lured him in, playing a slow and steady beat,
Little did he know, he was in for a nasty treat.

A roll of the dice, the game awoke,
Jumanji's roar unleashes its cloak.
With a mind of its own, a newfound beast,
Its deeds were dangerous, to say the least.

He thought that he could control it all,
But he couldn't resist Jumanji's call.
Vines engulfed him one limb by one,
Leaves encroached him till the damage was done.

Foxes encircled, cunning grin plastered,
Frogs croaked, a skill well mastered.
The chatter of monkeys, a lion's might,
Hawks swooped; crocodiles ready to fight.

Alex meets some friends to overcome the pain,
To face the challenges of Jumanji's terrain.

But problems they resolved and destruction they repaired,
The word 'Jumanji' echoes, ringing through the air.

Bulls on a rampage, elephants on a stampede,
A force that threatens, unable to retreat.

Neha Sabbella (13)

The Euros

In summer's heat, the passion wakes,
On fields of green where heroes break,
The air alive with chants and cheers,
A celebration through the years.
The Euros bring a nation's pride,
With hearts and hopes so amplified,
Each match a tale of skill and might,
A clash that burns through day and night.
The whistle blows, the game is on,
A dance of feet, the ball has drawn,
With every pass and every strike,
The crowd erupts in sheer delight.
From corners swift to headers bold,
The stories of the game unfold,
A drama played in coloured kits,
Where dreams ignite and legends sit.
A goal is scored, the net's embrace,
The roar of joy, a wild chase,
In every town, in every square,
The thrill of victory fills the air.
But not just wins define this stage,
The beauty lies in every page,
Of teamwork, struggle, and resolve,
The spirit of the game evolves.

The Euros, more than just a game,
A tapestry of pride and fame,
Where nations meet in fierce delight,
And hearts beat strong, and futures bright.
So here's to all who take the field,
To every joy and tear revealed,
In summer's glow, the passion grows,
The thrill of the Euros ever flows.

Zineddine Chennoufi (13)

Victorious

Eyes glow like torches as you bite the gleaming medal,
Eyes cast back at its shining surface,
Like a fragment of a star,
Now in your grasp.
The glory of failure had stoked your fire high,
The yearning to be the flame that carries on next time,
And reigning, at last, victorious.

The gods had chosen.

Eyes on the horizon.
Millions of eyes were on the horizon,
Brilliantly blue,
Spurring you on with shouts
Primal whoops,
Guttural roars,
With the eyes of the world on your back,
The sweet taste of victory,
Tantalising,
Urgent.
Almost there.
The scene played out in slow-motion
In the eyes of millions,
As the gilded laurel wreath glints upon your head
In the beaming sun.

The medal isn't worth just its weight in gold,
But years of work aiming for this priceless moment.
Fueled not by the prize,
But the journey to the top,
The getting knocked down almost worthwhile,
In order to pull yourself back up.
You hope someone in the crowd catches onto the spark
Of your victory,
And that they will coax it into something
Greater,
To become a star themselves,
The star that they always were,
And to be
Victorious.

Emma Dimitrova (15)

The Game Of Life

Life is the game we are all forced to play,
The game that we play every second of every day,
Except our moves are predetermined by a man in the sky,
Yet no one truly stops to ask why.

Why does He get to choose our starting position?
Who gave Him the permission,
To make the poor and the wealthy so asunder?
What was He thinking, what impression was He under?

Why does He get to decide the number we roll?
The dice is fixed completely under His control,
So the poor get a one and the rich will forever get a six,
For this game is full of cruel tricks.

Why does He get to establish how much money we get though?
Mostly decided by our family and who we know.
From the second you're born, you're reliant on luck,
Just hoping and praying you won't end up stuck.

Why does He get to conclude where we place?
Truly based on our gender, sexuality or race.
But life isn't fair and neither is this game,
For some things will forever be the same.

Life is the game we are all forced to play,
The game that we play every second of every day.

Except our moves are predetermined by a man in the sky,
And we are the pawns who never thought to ask why.

Amelie Mapstone (14)

The Struggle Of The Game

Some people find at a point in their life,
The days mundane, they wish to thrive,
See, we as people, we love a challenge,
We hunt down the prize, we sniff and scavenge,
We hope to play, we hope to beat,
To be the best, earn the feat.

We push and pull, lift and throw,
Battle and blunder our collective foe
An evil that lurks, the price of toil,
The tire that seeps; the work it'll foil,
Hold your breath, don't ruin the game,
If you fail now, no one else is to blame.

Running hurts but stopping's worse,
That inward war? An athlete's curse.
Don't give in to that human limit,
Reject that fear, eyes on the summit.
Steady breath, steady rhythm,
Leave it all behind, keep to the system.

You can see the end - it's getting near,
Time to lock in, you've been training for years,
If you just go faster, push some more,
You've come too far, won't settle for a draw.
Your lungs are cooking, clawing, crying,
But you need the win, your will is undying.

As you push to the end, you let that breath go,
You see the medal, what it'll show,
Your family and friends, their frowns deep set,
And then you see the winner, you try not to fret,
As your dreams all die, the game is lost,
But still next year, you will win at all costs.

Kelsey Jayne Balderson (16)

Games

Laughter fills the air, friends gather, ready to play,
Joy in every game; fun games for everyone,
Laughter spills in open air, joy dancing like sunlight,
Around the circle, friends gather with cards, dice,
Or just a ball, heartbeats race with each move,
Cheering, groaning, the thrill of the win,
Or the lesson in defeat.

Old ones, new ones, all shapes and sizes,
We dive into the challenge, holding memories
In every play, in the end, we find, it's not just the game,
But the moments shared, that make us smile.
In circles bright, where laughter fills the air,
A game unfolds, both simple and sweet.
With friends by our side, we gather without care,
Together now, our joys intertwine, complete.

A deck of cards, a dice's hopeful roll,
Each move gives a chance for stories to ignite.
We cheer for wins, share laughter as our goal,
In every game, a spark of pure delight.
From tag in fields where sunlight starts to fade,
To board games sprawled with snacks upon the floor,
Each moment spent, a lovely memory made,
In fun, we find what we are all here for.

So let us play, let cares drift far away,
In games for all, we shine in joy's array.

Lucy Jane (17)

My Favourite Sports

I love to play football and have won two football trophies.
However, I don't get to play it much,
As the boys in my class never pass me the ball,
And don't think I am good at football.

The role I am best at in football is as a defender,
Plus, it is my favourite role.
When I play as a defender,
And people see my defending skills,
They sometimes compliment me,
And say that I'm actually better than they thought.

I like football but don't like watching football,
Apart from my favourite teams, Arsenal, England and Italy,
On the television because it's not as fun to watch,
As it is to do,
However, I do like to watch football in real life.

I also love to swim as it's really peaceful and fun,
My favourite swimming position is being a dolphin
underwater.

I am really fast at swimming,
And I have tried out for the England swimming team,
But I didn't succeed because of my asthma
As I had to be way faster than I am to qualify.

My last favourite sport is netball,
I love making sure I make the ball miss
Getting to the other team player.
My favourite role is, once again, as a defender.

Mia Utting (12)

Summer School Sports

The weather is warm and the sun is out, shining brightly.
It is July, the last term of the school's academic year,
Which is jam-packed and lots of fun.
Ready, steady, go!
Ready, steady, go!
Get, set, go!
Get, set, go!
Summer Sports Day is about to begin!
Egg and spoon!
The egg and spoon race, relay race,
Sack race, the long jump.
Super fun, super school sports.
Scorching hot summer school sports.
Children excited to take part in the races.
Compete and complete summer sports.

S ack race

P aris Olympics 2024, children in schools are cheering on Team GB!

O bstacle courses are fun for families and for people of all ages. Also popular Sports Day activities

R elay running race - Run! Run as fast as you can!

T ug of war. Children, parents and school staff all take part and have fun

S uncream will protect your skin while you take part in super fun sports

D etermination and resilience are needed when taking part in competitive sports with school friends

A mazing teamwork takes place during Sports Day

Y ear R to Year 13, Sports Day is for everyone of any age.

Jennifer Nile (18)

Netball

The ball flies right past my face,
Zooming by, leaving no trace.
Grab the ball! Oh great, I missed,
I can't wait to send it flying with my fist.

Once again, the other team scores,
One more shot and we're starting wars.
The whistle blows as I dash for the ball,
Snatching it just in time - that was a close call.

Over their head, my team caught the pass!
But now wasn't the time to relax on the grass.
The opposing team blocked my team from throwing,
The pain in my legs was the only thing growing.

The ball bounced... into the hands of the other team!
The burning anger deep down intensified to extreme.
I blocked the ball's every escape - I wouldn't let this slide,
They attempted to throw, but the ball began to glide.

Whooshing down the court flew the legendary netball,
As the chances of them not beating us began to fall.
As I zoomed past, I managed to snatch it just in time!
In my head, the bells of hope began to chime

The weight was heavy, the pressure hit deep,
My eyes were still looking as the time couldn't sleep.

The hoop was there, this chance was my only slot,
1, 2, 3, the ball flew out of my shaky hands as I took my
shot.

Farah Karim (11)

Vengeance Is Sweet

A bead of sweat ran down my face;
Would it be spin or pace?
Oh, the grills are so awfully blinding,
And as I'm writing,
I can't forget rhyming!
For this beautiful game is all about rhythm and timing...

With an eagle's eye on the ball,
I have what it takes to hit them all!
That is what I told myself,
As well as that, I'll get that trophy on my shelf.

Oh, how it gleamed in its golden radiance of awe...
But now the bowler was running up from his mark.
The tattered seam was nowhere to be seen.
The atrocious trickster imprisoned in his greasy hand,
behind his back, you see.
He was no ace of diamonds, nor king of hearts.
He was but a mere joker who played his cards,
And his expertise kept me locked in the dark.

A blinding blur of red,
And leg, plum and off were dead.
They were once rigid - now battered and bruised.
My arch-nemesis celebrated as if he had performed a
stunning stunt like Tom Cruise.

But little did he know that I would bowl a toe-crushing
yorker to break his stumps.
And maybe a bone or two...

Ah, vengeance is sweet!

Indeed.

Riyan Mehmood (12)

Ode To The Champions Of Dreams

Beneath the torch's radiant gleam,
Lie tales of sweat and tears and steam.
Where dreams are forged on the anvil of hope,
And hearts beat to the rhythm of an Olympic slope.

In the arena where the brave dare to soar,
A symphony of endeavours, legends of yore.
Each stride, each leap, a ballet in time,
A pursuit of excellence, oh so sublime.

From the archer's poised and steady hand,
To the marathon's last, gruelling stand.
The discus dances in the azure sky,
While the pole vaulter aims to kiss it goodbye.

The weightlifter's grunt, the boxer's jab,
The equestrian's grace, the fencer's stab.
A canvas of victory, painted in stride,
Each stroke, a story of national pride.

For every fall, there's a rise anew,
A testament to the human spirit, so true.
The medals may fade, the crowd's roar may dim,
But the fire within shall never grow grim.

So here's to the ones who chase the sun,
Whose battles are many, but spirit, one.

May this ode to the champions, in verse, be spun,
For in the heart of the games, we all have won.

Leo Singh (10)

Each And Every Hit

Felt like a long time ago,
The world was a new place to me.
I can barely remember anything,
Apart from sight.
All my knowledge yet to burst,
And my energy yet to be released.

As time went on
Like a tree, I was growing.
And so my journey started,
And I was ignorant of
The battles yet to come.

It was all a test
Of my strength and longevity,
And how long I could last out there
On the court.
So I was on the road of life,
With bumpy lanes and a rough surface.

My load increased every passing year,
How twisted both lives were,
How tough they were to combine.
Is it worth it?
From problems in the classroom to the
Exhausting hours at the club,

The road was feeling bumpy,
Set to trip me up.

Competitions were varied.
Some felt like I was at Wimbledon,
But some, I was half-asleep on the court.
But I know it's worth it, as one day,
I could actually be slicing, smashing
Serves on Centre Court.

I hope later on the road,
I can make the most out of the racquet
And collect glorious gold
To add to my name.

Daniel Boyle (13)

I Like Summer

I like summer, it's really fun
To play with your friends out in the sun.

Whether it's sunny, cold or windy, that's alright,
Play some football or rugby and have a wee sip of Sprite.

Playing sports out in the sun
Like tennis or athletics, it is really fun.

When it isn't summer, I tend to mull,
It really ain't good 'cause rainy Scotland's so dull.

In the UK, it's normally bad weather,
So enjoy it while it lasts, before you know it, it will be
December.

At school, you will have sports day, for me it's already gone,
It wasn't good weather but it was still fun.

Not long left of school and before you know it,
I'll be in Primary 7, let's hope I don't blow it.

I wrote a poem a while ago and it got published in a book,
So I hope they say he's got real talent, and this one gets a
look.

For kids who like video games and playing inside,
It's not fit, nor athletic, not even a bit.

Your body needs fresh air and to get in some shorts,
So go outside, get active, and play some sports!

Finlay Paterson (11)

Netball Summer

In the summer's golden glow, the court awaits,
Where dreams are woven through swift-paced debates.
Netball's rhythm, a symphony so pure,
Where teamwork blooms and hearts endure.

On courts ablaze with passion's fire,
Weaving tales of grit and desire.
Fast feet pivot, a ballet in motion,
A game where strategy fuels devotion.

With every pass, a connection found,
In teammates' eyes, victory's sound.
From goal to goal, we race and strive,
In the thrill of the chase, we feel alive.

For ten summers, I've honed my skill,
In netball's realm, where time stands still.
From shooting hoops to fierce defence,
Each play a step, a forward tense.

Imagine courts where friendships bind,
Where victories sparkle, losses refine.
In every match, a lesson learned,
In every loss, a fire earned.

So in this ode to netball's grace,
In summer's games, we find our place.

Where passion blooms and spirits rise,
In netball's dance beneath the skies.

Mananya Kaur (14)

The Marathoner's Stride

Through dawn's dim haze, the runner bends
His breath, a whispered hymn, ascends.
The ground submits beneath his feet -
A steady beat that drums
The pulse of victory is profound,
And he still runs.
The cadence calls him back -
A symphony of grit,
Though muscles ache.
He heeds no pain, no limits bind his way,
For every stride dissolves the weight of day.

A gasp -
A stuttered breath - a fleeting hold,
Caesura carved in the air - then onward bold,
His lungs reclaim the wind,
His heart alight,
A furnace burning deep within the night.

The track extends an endless serpentine -
But through the bends, his focus sharpens keen.
With sinews taut, his will refuses a break,
He dances past fatigue, no moment's quake
Could shake his pace.
His spirit, iron-bound, defies the odds,
Transcends the weary ground.

And in the midst, the finish line is crowned.
With triumph bright, he breaks the ribbon clean,
A king of toil, through sweat and toil serene.

Khadijah Rahman (13)

Euro 2024

In summer's glow, with skies so clear,
The world will watch, the crowds will cheer,
As Europe gathers, one and all,
To celebrate the beautiful ball.

In Germany, the stage is set,
For moments fans won't soon forget,
From Berlin's streets to Munich's light,
The spirit of the game takes flight.

Teams assemble, nations proud,
Flags unfurl, anthems loud,
From group stage fights to knockout dreams,
Each match ignites with fervent gleams.

Players weave their magic spell,
With every pass and every yell,
The pitch becomes a battleground,
Where legends rise and tales are found.

In cities rich with history's gaze,
New stories form, old debts repaid,
The underdogs with hearts of steel,
The champions who make us feel.

From the first whistle to the final blow,
The Euros drama ebbs and flows,

With unity in fierce array,
In sport, together, we all play.

As summer fades and trophies gleam,
We'll hold onto this shared dream,
For Euro 2024 will shine,
A testament to sport's divine.

Sabiha Karima (4)

Fortnite Fun

In the summer heat when the day is long,
I grab my controller, where I belong.
In Fortnite's world, I dive right in,
A Battle Royale about to begin.

With friends online, we form our crew,
Building forts and dreams anew.
From dusty desert to lush green glade,
In this virtual world, no place is afraid.

Loot in hand, we loot some more,
Strategising where to score.
Storm clouds gather, we must move fast,
In Fortnite's game, we make it last.

Guns blaze, rockets fly,
Victory's near, I feel so high!
Building ramps, I reach the sky,
In Fortnite's world, I learn to fly.

But even in defeat, we laugh and cheer,
Respawn and try again, no fear.
For in this game, I'm not alone,
With friends around, we've truly grown.

So here's to Fortnite's endless fun,
In every battle, under the sun.

A world of pixels, laughs, and quests,
In Fortnite's realm, we're truly blessed.

Sehajbir Singh (9)

The Road To Glory

One team, one trophy, and one chance of glory,
This game would be the goal of my story.
Boots on, mind ready, and skills prepared,
We waited until our team was the first to be declared.
A light appeared, it brought our steps closer to the decision,
After this day, we would receive full recognition.
The start of the glorious game had commenced,
After all we did, it remained 0-0; we all felt tense.
The second half began and I felt a spark,
Our team was injured, everyone had marks.
But using all the team spirit, we did the impossible,
Everyone knew it was impossible, but we made it possible.
Holding the trophy was like a blessing,
Our loss was people's guessing.
Medals make me happy,
But wearing one made me happier.
The game is just a game.
Win or lose, it's just a name.
Sportsmanship is what's best,
As all of this is just a *test*.

Dhanusshan Ponnambalam (13)

Chess: The Poem

I am just a rook, free to move side to side,
I can go just about anywhere, to corners far and wide.
I can go to any square: 3S or 2B,
No other piece on the board compares to me.

I'm the noble knight, hopping over my friends,
You'll never see me coming - I'll make sure the match quickly ends.
I can pull off techniques beyond what you can see,
No other piece on the board compares to me.

I am the lowly pawn, I'm tiny but I'm strong,
With my unique abilities, nothing can go wrong.
My incredible techniques and strategies are key,
No other piece on the board compares to me.

I am the mighty queen, free as a bird,
When I capture your king, I'll shout, "Checkmate!" as far as can be heard.
If I'm captured, no worries, my pawn will revive me,
Because no other piece on the board compares to me.

Tom Foley (11)

The Sport That You're Made For

When you think about games, you groan or you smile
You say a quick prayer or you go run a mile
But it's not really about whether you're good or you aren't
It's are you doing the sport that you're made for?

When you think about games, you ask which type
You ask if you sit down or you need to get hype
But it's not about whether you get up or not
It's are you doing the sport that you're made for?

When you come to do games, stood up or stood down
You start without a smile and you frown
You've got to do it, it's for your own health
But to enjoy it, is it the one you were made for?

When you come to do games, stood up or stood down
You start with a smile, definitely not a frown
You don't have to do it, but it's for your own fun
And this is the sport you were made for.

Danielle Potts (13)

On The Cricket Pitch

On the cricket pitch,
With figures dotted all over,
Dressed in white, they didn't dare to even itch,
For they were playing on the cricket pitch.

Fielders' hands ready to catch,
Eagle eyes locked, heart pounding sounds,
Both teams craving victory tonight,
But only one will claim the winning crown.

In the bowler's eyes was a predator's gleam,
Months of training not to be in vain,
At the stumps, he'd set the daring dream,
A crucial ball to turn the game.

Batsmen's hearts beat in a rapid race,
As the bowler released the ball,
This could bring cheers or a fall from grace,
Destiny's decision in the fight.

Coach's knuckles white with fear,
Player's will pushed to the ultimate test,
Who will conquer? Victory near,
On the cricket pitch, passing the test.

Salih Mohamed Liyas (12)

Archery At The Olympic Games

Everything was laid out,
Over the idyllic evergreen gazes of wonderment.
Pure gold, arm straight out,
A bow overlapped the tail's end.
The determination; deprived a victorious grace,
Awaits, toned by compassion, demure,
And diligence flurries ecstatically, far and wide,
Just one dive to strive, a fight now awakens.
Writhing adorned the bow,
Meticulously plucked the thread
That unravelled the fragments of dexterity,
Resplendently shot into the eyes of gold,
Into the light seeping through,
As it seamlessly raved through the air,
Guiding the arrow through the passage of time.
To what yet awakens us,
Another conjuring dream upon the iridescent clouds.
Pierced an aureate aim.
Ranting and chanting came from behind,
A divine presence of one of a kind.
Awarded a one-of-a-kind something, unlike a dime.

Meredith Hulme-Spence (12)

Paralympian

People say they're not like us,
But I'm no monster with yellow pus.
A missing leg, I'm still human,
It won't stop me, sport's my passion.
Rich history, it's mine too,
A bit of recognition is long overdue.
And yes, I might be blind, so what?
I can still see we need a change of plot.
Listen to me, I must be seen,
I'm part of your world, always have been.
You might think I've just appeared,
But I've been here for years and years.
My body is different, but the rest of me's not,
I'm just another person, laughs, tears and snot.
Prosthetic limbs? Just a part of me,
They mean I can live more happily.
I love, learn and hope the same,
And just like you, I have a name.
And that name is not Disability,
Because that's just another category.
No, my name proves anything can be done,
My name is: Paralympian.

Gaïa Renverse Harris (13)

Basketball Mania

I love basketball,
And I hope I don't fall.
This is my favourite sport,
It all happens on the court.
As the ball bounces,
The spectator announces.
I try to take the shot,
From my spot,
I am very hot.
No luck this time,
But I am in my prime.
It's time to go again,
As I extend.
I catch the ball,
When it hits the wall,
Of the hall.
The whistle is blown,
And the ball is thrown.
Side to side,
With strength applied.
The ball is now back in my hands,
With the coach shouting commands.
I go to shoot,
Whilst in pursuit.

A flick of the wrist and into the hoop,
With a cheer from the group.
In it goes,
And through the hoop, it flows.
One win for us,
With a lot of fuss.
What an amazing game,
And that's how I came to fame.

Lilly Tyler (10)

Do I Care For Sports?

I never cared for sports
Until I saw the Olympics on TV;
The way the crowds cheered
Thousands roaring in support of one person.
My voice cheered too
For the event of my favourite hobby,
Skateboarding.

The competitors made their skateboard dance
They were in control,
On and off in seconds
Which inspired me to pick up my board
Maybe one day, the crowds would cheer for me.

For many years, I endured
Scraped knees and taunting mocks
Being called a fool.
My only comfort was watching the Olympics
And the respect everyone held for skateboarding.

Ten years later, still on my board
But this time, I made it
On TV, crowds cheering my name
Some were friends and family.

I won first place
Skateboarding
And realised, yes, I do care about sports.

Dannielle Amos (16)

Spain's Euro Glory

In the heart of the Iberian sun,
Where passion ignites like wild flames,
Spain's dreams unfurl,
A tapestry woven with hope,
Each thread, a story,
Each stitch, a heartbeat.

On the verdant fields of Europe,
They dance,
A symphony of skill,
Where every pass whispers
The promise of glory,
Every goal ignites the night.

With the weight of history,
They rise,
A phoenix from the ashes,
United in red and gold,
The anthem echoes,
A rallying cry in the air.

In the shadow of giants,
They carve their path,
A mosaic of youth and wisdom,
Each match, a brushstroke,
Painting a vision of triumph,
As the world watches, breath held.

This is Spain's campaign,
Not just the chase for silver,
But a celebration of spirit,
A journey through the beautiful game,
Where every moment counts,
And every heartbeat sings,
For the love of football.

Aydin Nasif (11)

Euro 2024 Football Game

The month of May came -
The beginning of the Euro game.
England, Poland, France,
All of the countries had a chance.
I sat down in front of the TV every night,
And invited my friends if they were polite.
Each team ran fast on the field,
Because of this, many goals were achieved.
Day after day, there was a football game,
Every day, someone went away.
I recorded carefully every result,
Because I expected my favourite team to become a cult.

The day of the final came,
England against Spain!
Every house in the neighbourhood waited,
The flag of England was waved!
First, second goal - everyone was shouting for joy,
And we were starting to enjoy.
But unfortunately, the final whistle,
Spain started to bristle.
All of Spain now celebrating,
With the Euro 2024 Cup waving!

Nikola Ivanov (8)

Opportunity

I have never been one for sports
And that much is true
I much prefer quartz
But what you like is up to you

Sports can vary from one to another
Like basketball and tennis
To cricket, rounders and football
Some people will say a sport is a hobby and that is true
But sports can do and mean much more to a person like you
Sports can make a person happy and brighten up their day
It could take a little of the stress away
It might bring back joyful memories of years ago
And show a smile that's bright and glows

A sport can distract you from life for a while
And show everyone a gorgeous smile

So next time someone asks to watch a match
Or play a game
Don't let the opportunity go away
Take it up
And have a go
You might surprise yourself, you never know.

Jessica Armstrong (13)

Selkie Sport

I am a selkie with an interesting game
We swim between islands, flipping boats
Us pups have to be careful to not take the blame
Our parents don't like it but still take notes

We swim up to sailors
None can catch us
None are our chasers
But they do kick up a fuss

The best part's the race as a seal
But there are orcas that lurk
And we can't become their meal
When I win, I give a smirk

I am the fastest and the best at shifting
But my voice is lower than the other pups
So when we sing, I lose, so enjoy listening
My least favourite song is the one about cups

It goes on forever, this race and this poem
I don't mind if I lose or win at this lark
This explanation was written on a whim
The one thing I hope is you don't see a shark!

Isabelle Penfold (14)

The Love Of Rugby

In the heart of the field, under the open sky,
A game of rugby, where spirits fly high.
Two teams in battle, with strength and might,
Under the sun's glare or the stadium's light.

The whistle blows, the game begins,
A test of endurance, may the best team win.
With every tackle and every scrum,
The echo of victory, a deafening hum.

The ball is kicked, it soars in the air,
Caught and passed with skill and flair.
Down the field, players dash and dart,
Each try scored, a work of art.

Mud on their faces, sweat on their brow,
They won't give up, they won't bow.
With grit and determination, they play the game,
In pursuit of glory, in pursuit of fame.

As the final whistle pierces the night,
Cheers erupt, oh what a sight!
Victory or defeat, it matters not,
It's the love of rugby, that's the thought.

Walter Ladwig (11)

Just In Time

Terrifying - the ball flying, thundering across the colourful
court
Breathing, shaking, tumbling, I make my advance
At last: turning, swiveling, dashing ahead
But it's too late - I just fall short.

The score taunts me behind my back, the menace.
Sweat tickles my temples as I give it my all.
Blindsided by booing and jeering, I stumble,
But have not lost. I disregard this detour to success.

Finally, I conquer my final peak. An electricity of ecstasy
Enraptures my body, I fall, I scream, my arms flailing in the
air.
Wimbledon won, I feel like I could leap to space and defy
gravity
And shake hands with the stars, miles above, who divined
my victory.

I play for the love of the game. I see my name unveiled on
the wall,
A list tall with the names of champions who came before
me.

Benji Williams (15)

Runners At The Ready

In London, where streets are far,
Stands the next shining star.
Will their determination become higher and higher,
Or will it be set on fire?

By the sound of a whistle, they go,
Racing through the city, row by row.
The crowd cheering loud and proud,
Now the annual race is on - Wow!

Makes the dream seem true,
When there's a light beam coming through.
The need for speed, makes you believe,
What they can achieve.

Through rain or shine, they press on,
Each step closer to the finish line,
Exhaustion grips, yet spirits soar,
In the London Marathon where legends combine.

The city's heartbeat, a rhythm of feet,
As runners conquer the daunting street.
In the race of passion and true desire,
They inspire, they accomplish, they conclude.

Chloe Rothwell (17)

The Figure Skater

Gracefully gliding across the endless stretch of white,
Her heart beats faster in the spotlight.
Millions of eyes stare down at the elegant skater,
She is a master of her craft, an inventive creator.

Smiling radiantly, she flips and loops,
As the dazzled, bewildered crowd cheers and whoops.
She jumps highly and her landings are clean,
A champion skater she is, a true ice queen.

She skates with poise, her movements art,
A true princess, she steals their heart.
Her spirals are long, her edges as sharp as a blade,
The rays of light reflect in her eyes, the colour of jade.

She fearlessly moves into the Biellman spin,
By now, the entire crowd wants her to win.
Her brunette hair curls, falling out of her bun,
One last twizzle turn and the dancer is done.

Laiba Sohail (15)

The Magic Of Sports

Ahhh, it's finally summertime,
Let's go to summer camp!
At sports camp, there are millions of children
From the neighbourhood waiting to start,
The first game we played was darts.
The winner of the darts was Dan,
He was happy because he was a fan.
Next, we did ping-pong,
Whoever lost had to sing-song.
In the middle of the box,
We saw a fox.
The winner of swimming said "When I was little, I always
dreamt about being the best at swimming."
At gymnastics,
All the girls were fantastic.
Before the game of soccer,
The ball was locked in a locker.
While we were cycling,
We picked up a lot of recycling.
The winner of tennis,
Announced he was going to Venice.
Last, we did bowling,
Which left us rolling.
Summer camp was fun!

Fabiola Zannini (8)

The Game

As the game arrives,
I feel my might.
I will fight.
To win the new high score.
I will win.

My heart pumps,
I have goosebumps,
But I don't care about the lumps,
I will win.

The game begins,
From the football to the swims.
From the start to the end,
Competitors dressed in a trend.
I will win.

Did you want to break me?
Did you think you really would?
Do you think you should?
But still, I will win.

As it comes to a stop,
The players are dropped.
The game is ending,
The scores are showing.
I will win.

I am a winner like my past ancestors.
I am the gift of hope.
I am victory, not like past history.
I will win.
I will win.
I will win.

Esther Yee-Yan Hon (10)

Try Them All!

In football, you kick the ball,
In rugby, you might trip and fall,
In cricket, you hit with a bat,
And pilates involves stretching on a mat.

But how do the balls feel about it?
Do they enjoy being smashed, bashed and kicked?
Do the bats enjoy it either?
Do they prefer pain, agony or neither?

Does the grass like being trampled upon?
Can it endure being stomped on?
Do the mats tremble with carrying the weight?
And is pilates really a piece of cake?

Do you want to hear the truth?
Well, they can't even feel it, not even the mat called Ruth.
They can't feel a single thing,
And they can't even hear a single *ping.*

So enjoy the sports and worry not,
Try them all, give each a shot!

Lois Kimnell (10)

Football

Football is the most satisfactory sport,
You shoot, attack, score and defend.
There are numerous rules in football;
There are offside fouls,
Which can lead to penalties or a free kick.
Cristiano is the G.O.A.T. and Pelé is a legend,
Messi is not the G.O.A.T. but he is pretty good.
England are in the Euros,
I hope we win.
We need to qualify,
We can't requalify.
We need to get to the second round,
We have to hit the rebound.
To score the winning goal,
We must avoid hitting the pole,
And secure our victory in the match.
Offside calls and penalties are in sight,
And moments of tension are under the floodlights bright.
They shoot, they score and they defend,
In pursuit of victory until the very end.

Esther Oderanti (11)

A Day In The Life Of A Gamer

It is the summer vacation
And the weather is not perfection
He woke up early and turned the toaster on
He finished breakfast and it was time to bond

The gamer went live and many players joined
They played fun games without spending a single coin
He was a bit tired but continued to go on
Then it was lunchtime, so his mum made him sirloins

It was noon time, and he went for a nap
He slept too long and he said, "Oh, drat!"
He panicked and went back to gaming ASAP
The other players just gave him a recap

It's 5pm and his dad made him a snack
He continued to play until the sky was all black
His eyes were tired and his mind was about to snap
Until he said, "Goodnight, it's a wrap."

Marcus Liam Castillo (10)

A Piece Of Toast

Playing games and doing sports,
Running with the hockey stick I bought,
Playing netball with my friends,
All the fun - it never ends.

Playing cricket on the field,
In my hand, a bat I wield,
The ball goes flying through the air,
I scored a six - that seems fair.

Playing football on the pitch,
Hoping to win, I have an itch,
The ball hits the back of the net,
Then it rained - the pitch was wet.

Playing tennis on the court,
Throughout this match, I have fought,
Hoping to score the winning point,
But it is a tie - our scores are joint.

Playing rounders in the square,
I'm not sure how I ended up there,
Running madly from post to post,
All I want is a piece of toast.

Maya Curtlin (14)

Hungry Hippo Tennis

Hello and welcome to Hungry Hippo Tennis
And just to warn you, the red one's a bit of a menace
It is Red and Yellow versus Green and Blue
And Blue hits it with such force, he knocks off Red's shoe
Next, Red hits it so hard, it's impossible to return and *boom!*
Hits Green in the face!
Red is so happy that he leaps with grace
Yellow is acting a lot like a clown
And then he hits it straight at poor old Mr Brown!
It's the end of the game and Red and Yellow won
Now they are chanting, "We're number one!"
Yellow and Red are through to the next round
And poor Green and Blue are weeping on the ground
Sadly, it ends here
But you can hear Yellow and Red celebrating and drinking
beer.

Tabitha Windett (9)

The Art Of Dance

To dance is to be free
To dance is to see
To see all the mysteries of the world
And find the truth unfurled
The lies spoken
The petite girls a token
To be collected
To be selected
For what they call glory
Whilst they travel through the pages of a very grim story
They stand on their tippy toes
And watch as people cheer from the theatre rows
Yet are still not good enough
They will go home in a huff
Practise their poise
How to land a leap with no noise
They will perfect each attribute
They will become absolute
Yet still try and try to reach goals they've surpassed
They will cry and shatter like thin glass
But to dance is to be free
They can dance but they can't see.

Jessica Pennington (13)

Dance Stereotyping

D on't say dancers should be skinny
A dancer can be any weight
N obody has the right to say that
"C over up," people say to dancers
E ating disorders are common among them
R eally, anybody can be a dancer

S ome people who are dancers hate...
T heir bodies as they are too skinny or too fat
E very dancer is perfect
R ed is the colour of their costumes
E ating disorders cause them to starve themselves
O n and off stage, they are being judged
T oo many dancers cry because of the judges
Y ou shouldn't stereotype dancers
P lease stop stereotyping people
E very dancer is perfect.

Sophie Siddle (12)

The Stadium's Echoes

The ball flies off the court,
The score, nought to nought,
The thrill of basketball can't be bought,
But the win is always sought

Another goal!
That just shattered the goalkeeper's soul,
The defenders can't do their role,
This football game just took a major toll

Tennis rackets clash,
As the opponents dash,
Across the court in a single flash,
Skill and speed in every smash

Bats swing, balls zoom,
Fielders chase with doom,
Cricket cheers fill the room,
In this game, joy blooms

In this stadium, everyone can unwind,
And watch their star players shine,
When the thrill of all sports combined,
Leaves their hearts racing, spirits entwined.

Zainab Iqbal (14)

Minnie

M innie was my best friend.

I loved football, and so did she! We even went to the same football club.

N othing could separate us - it was a match made in heaven. One

D ay, Coach said a member of the team would be promoted to a club for advanced players. I

G asped - this would be a dream come true! A week later, Coach called me over,

A nd guess what? He wanted me to join the advanced club! Excited, I told Minnie. But

M innie said he was being sarcastic. He was joking. Maybe I had

E ven made it all up. As I told my mum coming home early one Tuesday, soccer just wasn't for me.

S occer was for Minnie, who, two days later, was chosen for the advanced club.

Esha Hassan (16)

Rise To Glory

Glory comes from strategy
Beginning with training
Competing means doing it validly
Constant repetition is quite draining
Knowledge and skills are being gained.

I compete with the rival competition
In my multiple days of sports
My final event bringing me recognition
Many news agencies creating several reports.

I had won my race
Due to team encouragement
I have ultimately secured a place
I start feeling enlightenment
Sensing substantial pride.

My win was inevitable
For I had trained hard
I can be utterly unpredictable
The 100m only felt like a yard.

If you wish to achieve great heights
Then follow the passion inside your heart.

Eleanor Lancaster (15)

Football

On fields of green where passion reigns,
The game of football, it entertains.
With a ball at their feet, the players prance,
In pursuit of glory, they advance.

Strategising plays with skill and might,
They battle on, under Friday night lights.
Teamwork and dedication, hand in hand,
The spirit of the game, across the land.

From the roar of the crowd to the referee's call,
Football unites us, big and small.
It's more than just a game, it's a sensation,
Fueling dreams and sparking inspiration.

So let us cheer and celebrate,
The beauty of the game, so great.
Football, a sport that will never cease,
Bringing joy and unity, in moments of peace.

Kalen Noel (10)

Outstanding Olympics 2024

Busy boxers bouncing like mad hares boxing quickly.
Powerful punches thrown, stronger than a rainbow mantis shrimp.
Courageous cyclists bombing down winding hills like an eagle weaving through trees to catch its prey
Daring divers twisting tantalisingly around like a carousel
Stupendously swooping through the air like a ferocious falcon
Supersonic swimmers swiftly swimming like a speeding silver sailfish.
Perfectly poised on picturesque horses, proud to be peacefully prancing on parade.
Graceful and gentle gymnasts as light as a leaf on the breeze, but as powerful as a breaching humpback whale.
Robust runners propelling themselves off the starting blocks like Apollo Eleven charging through the atmosphere.

Charlie Wallace (7)

Paintball

Paintball is a sport, you know,
Where all the colours of paint flow.
Paintball is rough, paintball is tough,
Paintball is a sport where you can't get enough!

In paintball, you are armed in a big, heavy mask.
You think I know a lot? It's my dad, you should ask!
He once owned a team, his nickname was Snake,
They always used to play by the forest and the lake.

Back at the time, my dad was like twenty.
The paint bullets were hard, so he had bruises plenty!
And after hours and hours of endless fun,
He would complain to my gran, "My legs are so numb!"

But still, my dad has nothing to regret,
Because paintball is amazing, you never forget.

Patrycja Michalska (11)

Football Is Life

F ootball has lots of great players known as GOATs

O ne of the best GOATs is Lionel Messi

O ats are what they eat to stay fit

T raining is a crucial part of the game

B razil have won the World Cup five times

A ttackers have one of the most draining jobs on the pitch

L egends are born on the field

L ife is football

I deally, we wish we could all be Real Madrid rich!

S trikers are usually the best at shooting

L ife is football

I pswich play in the EFL Championship

F irst place is the best place in a tournament

E verything is better with football in the world.

Jacob Burton (10)

Spirit In Motion

In the arena of champions, they shine bright
In the world of Paralympics, they fight
Each athlete a warrior, with spirit so strong
Defying the odds, proving they belong

No disability can hold them back
Their determination never lacks
With hearts full of courage, they take the stage
Showing the world their unwavering grace

From swimming to track and field
Each event, a testament to their zeal
Sportsmanship runs deep in their veins
Resilient souls, free from chains

They inspire us all, these incredible stars
Showing us what true sportsmanship is
In the Paralympics, they outshine
Mountains they move, with strength divine.

Hafsa Muhammad Nusair (13)

Strawberries And Cream

Strawberries and cream, the most elite treat.
It is not only amazing to look at,
But it is most definitely amazing to eat.
With its plump, broad, curved shoulders,
That meet its pointed, narrow tip,
And the glossy red berry glazed with thick, rich cream,
Makes it a worthwhile trip to me.
The sun beams brightly over the court,
Giving me a tan that I did not ask for.
But why complain so bitterly about the silly sun,
When people have travelled far and wide,
To be seated in Centre Court?
Clutching onto my dearest dessert,
With my eyes intensely fixed,
On the professionals playing the game,
Oh dearie me! I best watch the match and behave.

Kenechi Ezeajughi (16)

All Or Nothing

I've always aimed for
Perfect tens in my life;
Compulsively, relentlessly,
I'd shoot my arrow,
No matter the circumstances;
Academically,
Visually.
But now, most crucially,
Athletically.
So many eyes pierce my form,
Like needles.
Now where my arrow lands,
The place, the chance, is narrow.
I've melded myself into an arrow.
The tip - a lethal, sharpened blade.
Everything crumbles if it's not a ten.
The judges hold my fate
In their hands.
What use are the wings of my arrow,
Without the courage to soar?
My bow is taut,
With a heavy breath
And the deafening silence
Of the crowd.

Lana Al-Taie (13)

An Ode To The Erdtree: Elden Ring

Erdtree, O Erdtree, lend me thy strength;
The path of the Tarnished is arduous at length.
To forge the Elden Ring, your Grace we are sent,
Erdtree, O Erdtree, lend me thy strength.

Strong foe ahead! The Tarnished proclaim;
Still, the beast ahead we seek to slay.
Coursing thy will through the strike of my blade,
Erdtree, O Erdtree, lend me thy flame.

Hark, the enemy is felled, we cry!
So free and wide are Limgrave's skies;
Time for greater battle as Fell Omens die,
Erdtree, O Erdtree, lend me thine eyes.

Caelid calls, we must become stronger;
New lands to conquer, maidenless no longer.
Skill is required, therefore I ponder,
Erdtree, O Erdtree, lend me thy wonder.

Aurelia Littlejohn (16)

Football World Cup 2022

Every grand competition has to come to an end,
And so does the mega event,
Football is just a few games away to get a new champion,
The unforgettable competition will make history,

When the ball touches the net,
Thundering roars come from the fans,
Mixed feelings,
Some crying,
Some yelling with joy,

When the final arrives, the hopeful world watches,
And the moment the ball is booted into the net on the winning penalty,
The world is rising higher than ever,
Like a rocket that's just taken off,

Finally, the moment the world was waiting for:
The new football champions are to lift their trophy!

Muhammad Umar (11)

The Rush

At the swish of a racket
A bead of sweat trickles down my cheek
This game will bury the hatchet
But at what cost will that be?

Movements are careful and controlled
As I prepare to strike
My heart plays a tune of growing hope
Despite my opponent choosing to fight

I dance around the court
Attempting to capture the thrill
Of green grass and world-class athletes
Armed with their uncanny skills

Scattered claps and held gazes
Both roaring and whispered praises
Channel strength into my thrash
A serve that sticks in ambitious minds
Releasing them from mental binds
And driving them to amaze us.

Emmie Hayward (14)

Poetry Games

Have you been wanting to do something fun this summer
but have no clue what to do?
Well, you're in for a treat!
There are ample things to do!

Do you like football?
Make sure not to fall!

Do you like tennis?
This game isn't for a menace!

Do you like rugby?
The game can get a bit dusty!

Do you like volleyball?
Please don't bawl!

Do you like cheer?
It seems like a fun career!

Do you like gymnastics?
Your body must move like rubber elastics!

Do you like to play board games?
Same!

Promise me you will do your exercise and play games.
Please don't play online too much!

Ayat Waseem Khan (9)

A Little Game Is Hide 'N' Seek

A little game is hide 'n' seek,
Hide 'n' seek,
Hide 'n' seek,
A little game is hide 'n' seek,
That I like to play.

When I hear the door go *ding*,
I open the door,
And let Còiseam in,
When I hear the door go *ding*,
"Hello! My name is Christina."

Christina counts and closes her eyes,
Closes her eyes,
Closes her eyes,
Christina counts and closes her eyes,
Còiseam runs to hide.

Còiseam runs and finds a spot,
Finds a spot,
Finds a spot,
Còiseam runs and finds a spot,
Then Christina finds him.

Christina Lucille Young (4)

The Rook

The rook stands guarded beside the king,
A silent force with a vigorous swing.
It moves on tracks both straight and true,
From end to end, it traverses the view.

When battles rage across the board,
And pieces crash with knight and sword,
The rook holds quick, a solid wall,
Its path is clear, its aim is all.

It knows its strength, knows its worth,
From its quiet start to a final burst.
A sudden strike across the way,
Can change the course and conquer the day.

The rook, a rock on black and white,
A silent tower in the fight,
It waits its turn and finds its mark,
A steady flame within the dark.

Sumera Arshad (14)

Chess

Black and white,
Bishop or knight,
Queen and king,
Wooden or plastic,
The pieces move like dominoes,
The board; a secret place that no one knows.

We are set on a time,
There is no grey line,
Each move has a consequence,
The air, always so thick and tense,
Be careful where you move,
Sometimes you can't go back.

All of us play,
This world of games,
In our head,
Or physically,
This world divides,
Nothing is equal,
People are smarter than others -
Machiavellian -
And it's fun,
When you know and plan out,
When you understand,
What you are looking at.

Eliza Ray (13)

The Shot Taken

From the tips of my fingers,
To the ground, hard against my feet,
A field is where I stand, arm straight,
Pointing across the sea to land.
Snake prey is my upper limb,
Scales protecting my mortal dignity
From the weapon I hold.
Breath is still as body is raised,
Twisted thread, nose just grazed.

Body in an automatic pull behind
As heaven approaches.
Retracing history, battles unbegun, laughter long
Arrows soar in harmony, melody and song,
Targets are as chromatic as the soldiers,
Striving for the centre.
Distances walked to get here,
Each person, their own inventor
Archery is my mentor.

Chloe Willcox (14)

Olympic Harmony!

Life is like a marathon, a race of strength and grace,
Athletes from all nations in one united place.
The Olympic flame ignites, a symbol shining bright,
Celebrating sportsmanship in the day and night.

With javelins and hurdles, and gymnasts in the air,
Swimmers in the pool with speed beyond compare.
The spirit of the Games, in victory and in defeat,
Brings the world together in harmony so sweet.

So let's cheer for the champions with hearts pure and true,
In the Olympic arena where dreams come into view.
May the Games inspire us to reach for the sky,
In unity and friendship, let the Olympic spirit fly.

Benjamin Doeteh (18)

1966

1966, what a time to be alive.
1966, the greatest goals of all time.
"Geoff Hurst scored!" everyone cried,
"The best cup win for years in line!"
Determined to win against West Germany,
England wanted to do this for you and me.
Blood, sweat and tears went into this game,
If we lost, it would surely be a shame.
Sir Hurst had other plans,
He was to be the first to score a hat-trick in a final,
This was his time to shine.
The minutes tick by, panic sets in,
Would Geoff be able to score again?
The crowd goes wild, the commentators roar,
This moment will be remembered for decades more.

Caitlan Bridge (14)

Dodgeballs In Space

D odging all that comes upon
O bjectives always new
D eviant but round, floating around
G oing away and coming back unexpectedly
E xecrable things can happen
B alls bigger than you think
A ll of the players are aliens
L osers go back home
L oving what they do
S pectators cheering for their team

I t isn't that easy
N iftier as you go

S eeing it is amazing
P opping balloons fill the air
A t the end, people see who won
C heering for the winners
E verything might go wrong.

Asana Draman (8)

The Dance Of The Kings

On the board, the armies will stand,
Black and white in command.
Pawns are in a quiet row,
The foot soldiers are marching where they must go.
Knights leap like thoughts, suddenly and bold,
Bishops tear through the secrets untold.
Rooks, like towers, are watching from afar,
They guard the queen, the board's brightest star.
The king moves cautiously, taking one step at a time,
He holds the heartbeat, the rhythm and the rhyme.
In each check and checkmate, stories unwind,
A battle of minds, where no one is blind.
Here, in this game where destinies meet,
Victory is next to impossible yet ever so sweet.

Sharon Saini (15)

Score Big!

Football is a sport,
Like many others,
Popular and fills up stadiums
But the thing you have to remember is,
Score big!

Basketball is a sport,
Like many others,
Five players each on a rectangular court,
Shoot the ball into a basket,
But the thing you have to remember is,
Score big!

Rugby is a sport,
Like many others,
A contact sport,
Running with the ball in hand,
But the thing you have to remember is,
Score big!

Sport is a competition,
Who is the best team?
A supporting union
Teamwork,
But the thing you have to remember is,
Score big!

Amelia Barnes (13)

The Spirit Of Games

In fields of green and courts of clay,
Where dreams rise with the light of day,
A thousand hearts in silent prayer,
The Olympic flame burns bright and fair.

Sprinters chase the fleeting line,
Swimmers dance in water's spine.
Gymnasts twist through weightless air,
Archers aim with focused stare.

Cyclists spin on roads that wind,
Boxers fight with iron mind.
Soccer's rhythm beats in time,
Weightlifters lift, defy the climb.

From every land, in every game,
The world unites in hope, the same.
Through every sport, in every feat,
The Olympic spirit is complete.

Deborah Adesanya (14)

Where We Shall Fight

In fields of green and courts of white,
Where athletes push with all their might.
The ball soars high, the crowds erupt,
In the game, we feel the deepest cuts.
With muscles strained and heart ablaze,
They chase their dreams through endless days.
A dance of skill, a battle fought,
In sports, our passions are all sought.
From running tracks to wrestling mats,
Where champions rise and fall like hats.
We cheer them on, we hold our breath,
In victory or bitter death.
So let us play, let us compete,
In victory or defeat.
For in the end, what matters most,
Is not the win, but how we boast.

Cody Garrett (9)

The Everlasting Flame Of Victory

Beneath the torch's glowing light,
Where nations meet and hearts unite.
The world, at peace, does firmly stand,
With hopes and dreams, all hand in hand.

Athletes pursue their goals of gold,
Through fields and streams, their stories told.
But win or lose, they all embrace,
The sacred bond within this place.

No walls divide, no borders claim,
Just human strength and burning flame.
In every cheer, a bond is made,
In every feat, our hopes cascade.

Though games may end and torches dim,
The light within won't fade or slim.
For in our hearts, the fire stays,
To light the world in endless ways.

Aaditri Manjunath (11)

A Little Bit Of This And That

A little bit of this and that,
A little bit of hockey and track.
The way I rapidly dash on the track,
The way I strike the ball on the field with no slack.
Speedily sprinting against the ticking clock,
The air pushing me back,
Tackling and dribbling the ball,
I ate that goal up like a snack.
Handing the baton to my teammates,
Working with my team to make the results great.
I love hockey and track,
They both keep my soul and me intact,
They made me realise skills I thought I lacked.
If you asked me what sport you should do,
I would definitely recommend hockey and track.

Khadija Aktar (11)

Football

There are lots of different sports but football is the best,
It is more fun than basketball and better than all the rest.

Football is my favourite sport, what else can I say?
It can be a lot of fun if you know how to play.

I watch the ball move to and fro,
Each player passing it like a pro,
For everyone to have a go.

Watching penalties makes the room fill with adrenaline,
You can never know who is truly going to win.

Even though we can't win every game, we will always have
fun,
It doesn't matter if we win or lose, our team will still be
number one.

Raeesah Khan (11)

Football

Football is really fun,
Although it makes me run.

My cousin has a game,
And when I play, I'm really lame.

She taught me how to save the ball,
And make a victory win for all.

I learned to defend and score a goal,
One time, I even met Ronaldo.

Do a dribble across the pitch,
And make the goalie start to glitch.

I played a game with Harry Kane,
It turns out, I drained his fame.

I'll run around, kick the ball,
Score a goal and win for all.

Soon, I woke up from a dream,
It turns out I wasn't in a team!

Ayana Khan (11)

The Best Of The Best

I was always the best of the best,
But it was nothing to the rest.

I always had to be the first,
I never wanted to be forced.

I stood out,
Without doubt.

And became the best,
Of the rest.

I pitched my tent on the crest,
Until the day I failed the test.

I felt my pride was stolen,
And now my face is swollen.

From the best of all the rest,
To the worst of all that's left.

"Hell no," I said,
And fought back to lead.

Here I am, happy with my choice,
For that, I always rejoice.

Chizzy Unachukwu (10)

Chess Lock

I knew it was a curse,
I was cursed to the board,
I tried to walk past,
But a thick dome closed,
So, I had to play...

I tried my best,
I really did!
I defeated every pawn,
Every knight, every turret-y thing,
The queen was easy,
But soon, only the king stood...

I closed in on him and his smirk,
And soon, his smirk would turn black,
Then I yelled a powerful word...
"Checkmate!"
Lightning brought me back to my normal size.

The moment I won was like an award,
But I'm glad I am off that chessboard.

Emiline Anderson-Kalsi (11)

Swimming Race

Perched at the edge of the pool,
I stretched up and made myself tall.
With the fire of the gun,
This would be so much fun!

I quickly dived in,
Surely this was my chance to win!
As I stared at the bottom of the pool,
My heart started to race!
I was going fast but at my own pace.

As I noticed the water got colder,
I developed an ache in my shoulder!
I just couldn't give in,
My limbs were flapping like a fin!

Ahead, I saw the finish line,
This was now my winning time.
The big shiny gold medal,
Was finally all mine!

Isla Eves-Davis (9)

Sports

I like the Olympics,
In football, they do lots of tricks.

In football, you do lots of kicks,
Sometimes you do gymnastics.

People like playing with a ball,
Football defenders should be tall.

In lots of sports, you run,
While you're playing, you have fun.

When I play football matches, I have won,
When I play with Daddy, I am number one.

To get strong, you don't leave food waste,
To keep healthy and strong, brush with toothpaste.

People like playing when it's sunny,
When people miss, I find it funny!

Toby West (6)

Chess

You can't be second in chess,
Unless you make a mess.
You have to watch every piece,
As you never know the opponent's next move,
All eight pawns potentially becoming queens.
You can't be second in chess,
It's a lot like real life.
One wrong move and it's over,
You need to be like a soldier;
Observant, quiet, brave,
You don't want to sacrifice your
Queen, rook, knight or bishop
Unless you know that's how
You will checkmate your opponent.
As long as you're not second in chess,
Because you made a mess.

Evie Ansell-Rodgers (16)

Showjumping Dreams

Some say that riding isn't a sport,
I say it is,
Some say we just sit there,
I say we ride,
Over the poles, our horses leap,
We count our strides between the jumps,
Remembering the order of the course,
Focused on what we have to face,
Cantering gracefully,
Each hoof that touches the floor is one step closer,
Up ahead is the next post,
Picking up speed,
Heading towards the centre,
The crowd goes silent,
A small thud as we land safely,
The claps and cheers return,
Bringing confidence and pride,
Showjumping is a sport.

Zoe Worth (12)

United

People travel above and below, fast and slow:
To all the many places one can go.
To see the Euros, World Cup and Olympics too,
But what makes these things special is what's within you!
Whether it's your love for football or your joy for cricket:
Everybody's dying just to get a ticket!
Oh, what fun it is - I really am starting to get the gist:
Football fever, cricket craze, basketball bonanza, hockey hiccups -
I am just amazed!
Too many things we are united by,
Too many things one can do,
But what's special is what's within *you!*

Ahana Madhok (10)

The Football Competition

Everybody was born ready for this day,
Their legs were as tight as skinny jeans,
And their heads were in the game,
As the polished ball rolled and rolled,
It crossed the pitch from left to right,
The smooth ball made a satisfying flick,
As it hit the back of the rough net,
Many people roared and cheered,
While the others booed and cried,
It was as competitive as a radiant race,
But at the end of the game, one team lost,
While the others turned that frown upside down,
I guess that's why it's called the football competition!

Fareedah Adenusi (10)

The Route

As I advance delicately
Mentally following the route
I appreciate the scene ahead
My eyes meeting the beautiful silhouette

The hills that lay before me
Presenting their vibrant green colour
Surrounded by a canvas
Of the gleaming azure sky

Gently, I feel the breeze on my face
As I start to make progress
Through the route of the Tour de France

The Alps covered in snow like cooking powder
The sun beaming on me like a torch
The mountains giving me a sight for sore eyes
Is all part of the Tour de France.

Sky Lawton (17)

Some Save Lives

To love a sport,
Is to love music,
Is to love a subject or an item.
It's to eat, sleep, do sport, repeat
In their world.
I knew a boy once,
He hurt so bad, his sport was gone.
Not forever, but so much happened in such little time.
You feel so empty, so bored,
Like there's nothing to call home.
It drives you crazy,
When there's nothing there to amaze you,
And people say it's just a sport,
But no one ever really understands,
The physics of when someone loves something
So much that life is just a fan.

Gracie Chapman (14)

The Roller Coaster Of Sport

Adrenaline gushes into veins,
Silence conquers in the final minutes,
It's all a trial of disappointment or glory,
A fire of tension ignites in eyes,
Storms of anticipation whirl and thump against hearts,
Each grain of time matters,
A hope of pride, joy and triumph,
A World Cup dream,
A roller coaster athletes survive,
Footballs fly through the air,
Tennis balls glide over nets,
Cricket balls score sixes,
A team goes home with a breathtaking victory,
Cheers go off like fireworks,
Happiness plastered on their faces.

Shreekant Baravkar (10)

Summer Of 2024

2024 is one year you won't forget,
By sitting on the Olympic podium eating a baguette,
Or watching tennis players on the grass breaking a sweat,
We all had so much fun,
If that was viewing the Tour de France under the sun,
Or maybe even going out for a run,
The heat was high and so was the happiness,
Many enjoyed playing all the sports from badminton to dancing,
Horse riding to kayaking,
Lots had joy staying at home,
And playing a good game of Scrabble,
2024 is the best it could be,
And I hope you all had an amazing summer.

Ananya Sanil Balakrishnan (12)

Going For Gold

She felt that fear would tear her apart,
When the whistle went, courage came to her heart.
Off she raced, as fast as lightning,
She fell behind but kept fighting.
She overtook second place,
Almost at the end of her race.
With one more person to overtake,
She kept on going without a mistake.
She raced around the track and began to fly,
Was this race going to be a tie?
On she went, sprinting around the bend,
At last, she was at the end!
As she waited, she stood strong and bold,
She was given the medal and it was gold!

Eilidh Graham (10)

Always Protect Your Queen

I have only recently started to learn how to play chess.
I must confess, it's my favourite board game!

Here's what I've learnt so far...
Never underestimate the pawn.
The piece with the horse's head and neck, aka the knight,
can be quite tricky.
The bishop is a long-range piece and can be very powerful.
I love that the rook can move as far as its line of sight.
I rely on the queen to protect my king.
But only the king bows down to his queen!
It's a bit like my life, Mum's my queen and I'm her king.

Joshua Otalor (5)

Anfield

Anfield, Anfield,
When do we meet?
Anfield, Anfield,
When do we greet?

It feels like I can hear the crowd already,
It looks like they are excited and ready.
I can feel the energy and vibration within me,
I can hear their songs and the melody.

It is a dark and rainy night,
The opposition looked scared with fright.
No one can beat this team of champions,
Because tonight they had given us satisfaction.

I look to the sky with hope and desire,
When do we meet, Anfield? It is all I aspire.

Raihan Farooq (13)

Wimbledon

You enter London very bold,
You walk into the stadium all grey and cold,
Get your racket ready, you're about to play,
Tie your shoes up, they might get in the way,
Spectators' heads going left and right,
Don't get distracted, you must play with all your might,
As you do your signature tennis growl,
Your opponent calls a game foul,
You look all innocent and confused,
The umpire disapproved,
As the ball bounced,
You did a large pounce,
Finally, the game is done,
I wonder, *who won?*

Elsie Rich (10)

Flying

This is the closest you can get to flying,
Whizzing down the mountainside,
The sound of crushed ice and snow beneath my feet.

This is the calmest I can ever be,
Going off-piste,
An endless sky effortlessly stretching out before me.

Now, here is my favourite part,
Sitting on the lift,
Waiting for the next part of the landscape to unfold like a
pop-up book.

Now, my brother is nearly old enough,
18 months in fact,
To learn how to stand on two wooden planks,
Now, I can share the magic.

Lily Wall (12)

The Game Begins

Everyone didn't know what football was
Until one day, some boys made a ball out of plastic bags
And started throwing it around.
Then one of them kicked it and everyone was shocked.
They made a new game
And thought about what they should call it.
They thought about it and called it football
Because you kick it with your foot and it's a ball you use,
So they put foot and ball together to make football.
It is now a very popular game that everyone loves to play
And watch their favourite football team.

Ryan King (15)

Embarrassing England

Oh England, oh my homeland,
Why did you lose? You're on a cruise.
Back home, remember the times
When you used to roam.

When you were in your prime,
Those were the only good times.

Now, Harry Kane is old,
He can't score any goals,
So now he's plain.

Southgate leaves,
So all the England players skate on thin ice.

We are going to lose every game,
Unless Pep comes in,
And gives England a quick step forward.
If not, England shall see the doorstep.

Hafsa Nasir Choudhry (10)

Heart Of The Game

Palm trees sway in the wind,
Sun glares off the windshield, blinding passersby,
The Hollywood sign stands tall and proud.

Lights flicker on and off,
Moss placed perfectly on each brick,
Nothing seems out of place to passersby.

All is perfect,
No way anything could go wrong,
But a slight glitch,
And all could blow like a bomb.

A heart is like a video game,
Built up, level by level, perfectly,
Yet broken by the slightest glitch,
Just one error, and it's game over.

Matthew Heeks (13)

The Mystery Sport

Like many sports, I have a smooth, round ball.
And like a select few, it is fairly small.
Can you guess what I am called?

I have no hand-held racquets or a hip-high bat.
I am not played inside or on a soft, plush mat.
There are no hoops or loops and you can't change that.

I do have a thin stick, which is long with a curve.
To piece it together, the clues you must observe.
If you get it right, a reward you deserve.

Have you guessed me?
Let us see!
I am... Hockey!

Nia Roberts (10)

160

Cricket

Cricket is fun,
But you really must run.
Sadly, it's not the king of sports,
But it doesn't have half-courts.
Some people would say that,
Well, those people are bad.
In cricket, you can hit fours or sixes,
Like Suryakumar Yadav who mixes.
A famous stadium is the Wankhede Stadium,
Which isn't made of ferrovanadium.
Sachin Tendulkar is the little master,
And the father of another cricketer.
That's a short summary of cricket,
Now I'm going to have a biscuit.

Kartik Kamble (9)

Lords: Day One

Down at Lords,
Birds chirping away,
Filled up with hordes,
Hoping for good play.

England vs West Indies,
A spectacular game awaits,
Promised Crawley fifties,
And from captain, Kraigg Brathwaite.

England opening the batting,
With Crawley and Duckett,
Crowds cheerfully chatting,
Bets being made on this game of cricket.

Expected 300+ from England,
But West Indies bring on Seales,
Swinging into the stumps,
Knocking them over, Duckett: golden duck.

James Edwards (12)

An Olympic Dream

Standing on the starting block, ready to dive in,
Quick look at my family before the race begins.
The whistle blows and in I dive.
One, two, three, breathe,
One, two, three, breathe,
One, two, three, breathe,
Ready for the tumble turn as I approach the wall.
One, two, three, breathe,
One, two, three, breathe,
One, two, three, breathe,
I'm nearly there, faster, faster.
My fingertips touch the wall.
Who touched first?
Could it be?
Is it possible?
Gold!

Noah Murton (10)

The Hardest Game

What is the hardest game? I think to myself
Is it football or the chess on my shelf
Basket or volleyball
High jump or a boxing brawl

But the hardest game is life
It's full of all this strife
Never a straight, unbroken path,
To call it easy invites a laugh.

Life's a game you are here to play
It doesn't always go your way
Don't hate the player, hate life's game
Because if you don't play the right way
You will never stay the same.

Ibukun Durojaiye (13)

DribbleVerse

DribbleVerse on the court so grand,
Spinning tales while the ball's in hand.
Bouncing rhythms, a poet's delight,
In the game of hoops, shining bright!

In the realm of bouncing balls and soaring dreams,
On the court where passion gleams,
Players dance with skilful grace,
In a game where hearts race.

So let the echoes of the court resound,
In every bounce and every bound,
For in the poetry of basketball's art,
Lies the beating of a champion's heart.

Bridget Frimpong (17)

Sport Is For Everyone

Playing sport - everyone wants to win,
Passing the finish line makes you grin.

Team sports bring people together,
Supporters are united, whatever the weather.

Whether you have one leg or two,
You can compete with someone like you.

Whether it's live or at home,
On TV or your phone.

Swimming or cycling, running or hiking,
You can find something to your liking.

Players and fans all have fun,
Which just proves sport is for everyone!

Hazel Foster (10)

The Swimmer

With my hands above my head
I was so focused on the wave
I dove into the water
My dream had been made
Swimming fast and rapid
I was truly trying my best
I was now in third position
This was no time to rest!
I went from second to first
As my hand touched the end
I had done it! I won!
The other swimmers rounded the bend
And as I stood on the podium
A medal, shiny and new
Was given to me
I was filled with joy
My Olympic dream had come true!

Olivia Dodimead (9)

Anfield

When I play at Anfield,
I'll hear the Kop roar!
Winning a shield,
A dream no more.

I once played football,
On a field.
In hopes of a Ballon d'Or,
And a contract sealed.

Fans chant a hero's name,
Scoring goals,
And gaining fame,
Keeper staring into my soul.

Making defenders turn to stone,
Stands sing so loud, they're heard in Mansfield.
Dribbling 'round the training cones,
When I play at Anfield.

Ryley Patterson (12)

Sports

Sports are my favourite thing,
But it used to be so hard.
I was scared to start a running race,
But now I can run so far.
There are so many types of sports,
As many as could be.
Hurdles, long jump and sprints,
So, do you see?
Volleyball, basketball, baseball,
Are there any more?
Also football, Euro 2024!
Oh, there's netball, badminton,
And, of course, can't forget about swimming,
It used to be so hard, but now I'm always winning!

Ambar Javed (10)

Life Of The Amazonia

Life of The Amazonia is my favourite game,
To build a habitat for your animals is the aim.
You should put a frog next to a lily pad,
Because if you don't, it will be mad.
Put your woodpecker next to a tree,
Then it will be happy, that's a guarantee.
Your caiman wants lots of water plants,
You have to give him lots or you won't stand a chance.
Toucans want trees and your otter wants land,
You can buy both of these with leaves from your hand.

Evelyn Hardy (12)

The Competition

In the heat of competition,
We push our bodies to the limit.
Sweat pouring down our faces,
Heart pounding with each movement.

The thrill of the game,
The surge of excitement,
Brings us together as a team,
And makes us feel alive again.

From the thump of the bat,
To the roar of the crowd,
Sports ignite a passion,
You cannot just keep it under control.
It is not just the one game; it is all the games.
Play never stops.

Larissa Gray (12)

Cricket

Cricket is the game
Eleven people in a team
Invented by the English
No doubt, it's my favourite

Cricket is old, played by Saxons
And now by everyone
Cricket is modern; they play tests
And now one-day and T20

When sixes and fours are hit
Everyone's heart races
When wickets are down
Everyone's mood is down

Wides and no balls
Nobody wants to see it
Jumps and catches
Not everybody can do it.

Athmika Jeyakanth (10)

A Swimming Star

When I swim, I like to win,
It always gives me a great big grin.
Lane one, lane eight, never hesitate,
Soon, it will be the time to celebrate.
But how did I get here? Never fear,
I'll tell you now, my magic idea.
It's about working hard and playing hard,
It's what I know can make me go very far.
Of course, to succeed, I must not flop,
Or do I mean belly flop?
So come on, everyone, get behind me
And cheer me on to the very top.

Emily Garrett (10)

Five Nights Of Gaming

I start up my console, I'm nervous but ready,
I'm joined by Chica, Foxy, Bonnie and Freddy.
Five Nights at Freddy's is my favourite game,
Most of the kids my age feel the same.
It's set in the pizzeria, an old shut-down place,
With bright neon lights and a load of cool space.
Freddy, a bear, is sure to give you a scare,
Bonnie the bunny is anything but funny,
Chica looks sweet but she is no treat,
And Foxy will give you a fright!

Logan James Jones (9)

Confidence

As she entered the Olympics,
Her heartbeat began to rise,
Will she win the tennis match,
Or will she begin to cry?

As she picked up her tennis racket,
Her heart filled with joy,
Will she lose the gold,
Or will she win it all?

The match starts,
After a few deuces,
She eventually loses,
No gold for Carinda.

When she lost,
She felt shocked,
But she realises,
It's the taking part that counts.

Gracie Peach (10)

Game On

His best-ever finish is seventeenth place,
He will never win any race.
But don't give up, you've still got luck,
Score that goal in that net,
So winners win their lucky bets.
Swim with the school,
Swim the Channel, swim like a sea mammal.
Find your place and get your pace,
Feel the wind blow in your face,
Running past the crowd with grace.
Now, let's see which number you placed,
You have taken part and that is just ace.

Lily Bayliff (10)

Ice Skating

Swanlike, gliding
O'er glassy sea,
Graceful, elegant,
Perfect harmony.
Symphony of spins and leaps,
As beautiful as can be.
Stepping softly,
Cool as the ice they tread,
Slips, falls, tumbles
These mishaps, they never dread.
Serene, as though on solid ground;
The dancers begin their waltz;
Boots as white as purest snow,
Blades that shine like gold,
The figures, gifted, statuesque,
The ice ballet unfolds.

Katherine Clough (14)

Football And Me

Before I could crawl, I could kick a ball.
When I was two, I put on my first football shoe.
When I was three, you could kick it back to me.
When I was four, I could score.
When I was five, I wanted to thrive.
When I was six, I could do fancy tricks.
When I was seven, I got scouted - I was in heaven.
When I was eight, I could not be late.
When I was nine, it was my time to shine.
Now that I'm ten, I want to do it all again.

Teiarnie Moore (10)

Dance Reality

Dance is what I think about,
It's what I dream about day and night.
It's like you get to share a gift with others,
And it's truly magical.
It has a variety of styles,
That brings a variety of smiles.
In acrobatics, you leap into happiness,
Ballet takes away your sadness.
Tap helps you step into a new reality,
It develops a new individuality.
Amateur or professional,
Your moves will always be exceptional.

Victoria Cicha (16)

A Kid's Imagination

Dogs flying on unicorns, having a blast,
Monkeys Irish dancing, moving so fast.
Cats wearing bow ties and fancy suits,
Big hairy gorillas sit playing with their flutes.
Cows in tutus twirl around,
Whilst stripey sheep bang on the drum,
Gosh, what a sound!
Dancing donkeys spinning around,
Until they all fall to the ground,
Strictly's not just for celebrities,
As my imagination has just found.

Lilly Woosnam-Jones (10)

Eyes On The Pitch

Anticipation brewing, I put on my kit,
Dash down the stairs and switch on the game.

Eleven players emerge from the tunnel,
Belting out the anthem,
More than a team, proudly a nation.

Smell the anticipation, taste the excitement,
Drink in the atmosphere, wide-eyed with suspense.

A final huddle, positions taken,
The shrill of the whistle blows.
Kick-off,
All eyes on the pitch.

Lenny Wyatt (10)

Sports Are Fun

S wimming is lots of fun
P laying tennis in the sun
O ver the pole in high jump
R unning and sprinting
T iggers going really fast
S winging on monkey bars

A ll our muscles working really hard
R acing other people
E veryone playing games

F lying high when you jump
U K charity runs
N ever stop doing sports!

Emily Howitt (7)

The Four Olympics

Haiku poetry

The Olympic Games,
Where people will clap and cheer,
For those taking part.

Skiing and skating,
Are present in the winter,
When snow is falling.

Tennis and swimming,
Are present in the summer,
When the sun is out.

Paralympics too,
For the disabled athletes,
Who are brave enough.

The Youth Olympics,
Are available for young,
Who want to be stars.

Amber Sedighi (11)

Olympics

O   lympics, what an occasion!
L   ooking for a champion, whether they're British, African or Asian
Y   oung and old, trying their best
M   any hope to win, to complete their quest
P   eople run and people cheer
I   ncredible athletes see the finish line near
C   redit lies with the winners, it isn't lacked
S   oon, in a few years, I'll be the one on that track!

Philippa Julian (10)

Fiona The Meringue Climber

Fiona the meringue Olympian
Crispy on the outside
Soft on the inside
Olympics of fun
Splash and swim
Jump and run
Fire and torch
And lots of fun

Punching and flipping
Throwing and catching
And so much climbing
And you always
Need your timing
At the end, I won a gold
I went home
And got told that I am
A crunchy, munchy, crispy
Soft meringue.

Isla Longden (10)

Hockey

Hockey is my life, I've done it since I was five,
Rain, snow, sun, the game must go on.
Training in the freezing cold got us working hard,
Academy on Thursday too, what should I do?
Work hard, play hard, get through the pain,
We are a squad and we train, train, train.
Sunday is our training day, but it is also a fun day,
Where our whole club comes together and...
Plays the hockey game!

Ava Clark (12)

It's Coming Home

I'm in the team.
Thrilled to play. I won't let them down.
So happy, I made it.
Coming out. Scarves waving, fans singing, hearts beating.
Okay, it's about to start.
Missed! That was our chance.
It's gone.
Nervous, I need to play.
Goal!
Hold on, nearly there.
Over.
Made it.
Everyone's together. We finally won. It's coming home.

Ava Knighton (8)

Olympics

O nly happens once every four years
L ots of people are joining in
Y emen to Afghanistan, many countries take part
M edals can be won, gold, silver and bronze
P eople are doing lots of different sports
I like watching the swimming and the diving
C heering helps the athletes to keep going faster
S omeday, I would like to be in the Olympics!

Harry Pearson (6)

Rocket Racing

In this sport, you race in rockets,
You fight and drive for glory,
You can't tip over or lose,
Oh, and it's such a story.

You do maths in your rocket,
So you know where to go,
You can run and jump so you win,
Also, you can shoot with a bow.

And when you get to the end,
You find out that it was a dream,
But you don't mind,
You just gleam.

Harrison Farmer (9)

A Challenge Or An Opportunity?

A challenge or an opportunity,
Facing negative comments on social media,
Missing in a penalty shootout after being chosen.

A challenge or an opportunity,
Being selected for the finals,
Standing against a great enemy.

A challenge or an opportunity,
Facing a fear,
Being given a choice, a chance.

The question is:
Is it a challenge or an opportunity?

Jennifer Jenkins (12)

Playing With Fire

F or me, it's the thrill of movement
O n the field, my eyes are stuck with amusement
O ther teams against mine is a chosen war
T hen watching them, my legs are sore
B etting on our team, what are they trying for?
A nd then we roar, "Score!"
L ive, love and laugh: England won!
L isten to us laugh and we watch you mourn!

Suhani Das (13)

Crossing The Line

The whistle blew,
I could see the line,
Everyone started to run,
Before my eyes.
I'm not sure I can make it,
My legs are like jelly.
I can hear the cheers to run faster,
Just a few more steps,
Keep going, I tell myself
I could see the finish line,
I could see everyone crossing it,
Maybe I won't be last,
I just want to make it.

Hope Miles (9)

Summer

Every morning, I come out and play
Whether it's a sunny or rainy day
I hang out with my cousin
And sometimes we play badminton

Instead of going to stores
We enjoy our time outdoors
Playing badminton for half an hour
It boosts our energy and power

So instead of staying inside
Why don't you have fun
And go outside to meet the sun.

Syeda Anisa Mumtaz Nakvi (11)

Footgymming

There are lots of sports around the world,
But the one I'm talking about has never been heard.
A mix of gymnastics, swimming and football too,
A sport that is fun for me and for you.
Footgymming is fun for all,
Do tricks to get the ball.
Swimming in water is key,
Gliding past as fast as can be.
To score a goal, kick it in the net,
Who wins the game is anyone's bet!

Arianna Fordyce (7)

I Like Playing Football

I like playing football
On Wednesdays after school
I put my Chelsea kit on me
I listen to what they say to do
Learning dribbling and running with the ball
My favourite thing is when I score a goal.

Football is tricky
I concentrate and try my best
I want to be like Cole Palmer
And play for Chelsea one day
I like playing football.

Oaklee Dando (5)

A Poem About Sports

Sports, sports,
They are too complicated,
Sports, sports,
They are my favourite.

They sometimes don't look like one,
Feeling just like badness,
Like beanbags, cup stacking,
And hula-hoop madness.

Sports, sports,
Everyone goes crazy,
Sports, sports,
Don't be lazy.

Everyone,
Cheers for a team,

Ayra Jamal (9)

World Of Sport

Close your eyes,
Hear the racquets hit the ball,
Look at how they score a goal,
Sportspeople are artists.

The way they skilfully score their goal,
How tennis players artfully hit the neon ball,
The way basketballers pass the ball,
How runners run at light speed.

Now open your eyes,
It's the end of our adventure.

Beatrice Elizabeth Matiukhina (9)

Fortnite

F orts are built high in the sky
O pen fire when you desire
R evive your team; if you do not, then that is mean
T eamwork makes the dream work
N ever underestimate someone's ability
I t is always better to play with friends
T o win or not to win, that is the question
E veryone is supreme.

Joshua Brown (13)

My Pitch

F ootball, where passion and the play is real
O n courts of green and fields of gold
O n the pitch, each pass and tackle
T he rush of wind, the whistle's call
B oundless joy shapes my day
A rhythm that no time can steal
L eaving my heart on the pitch
L osing myself in every win.

Pareeza Umar (12)

My Favourite Sports

Badminton,
Cricket,
Tennis and golf,
Volleyball and boxing,
Here we go!

Rugby and baseball,
Hockey and football,
Swimming and climbing,
Biking and hiking,
Watch me while I'm riding!

Basketball and dancing,
Handball and softball,
Figure skating, ballet,
These are my favourite sports!

Sukhman Kaur (8)

Gymnastics

Double backflips in the air
Now I see why people care!
This Olympics has been the best
But I'm a boxer (worse than the rest).
This gymnastics surprises me
As they walk back in a three...
Double handspring!
What a show, now I feel I must go
I could never beat such an act...
Without boxing gloves!
I'm back!

Elika Rafiee (9)

Careful Moves

Eyes narrowed and fingers poised,
Watch innocence of the poker face,
Settle on fair and calculating queen,
Gradually place upon the square of truth,
Knights and bishops to answer the attack call,
Protect the frail king from harm,
Opponent expressionless,
Then, with the swiftness of confidence -
"Checkmate."

Edie Cook (14)

Basketball Challenge

Tick-tock,
Watching the clock.
Time passes by very quickly,
Will the match ever end again?
Whistle blows, half-time; phew, a break.
Basketball is hard. I have trained hard.
Next half, I start strong with 25 points.
The Bulls only have 10 points,
They are behind by a lot.
The whistle blows.
We win!

Florence Reed (11)

My Sports

Haiku poetry

Fast swimmers swimming,
Gymnasts performing their best,
Olympic players.

Amazing football,
Countries compete for the cup,
This is the Euros.

All tennis players,
Compete against each other,
It is Wimbledon.

Sports are really good,
These are all my favourites,
Sports are amazing.

Esha Raheel (10)

Football

Football is a great sport
But that is what I thought
Until I was a player
I loved to watch Demon Slayer.

In the game, I was loved
But then I got shoved
And I hurt my head
So I lay in my bed

Unable to move
Then I was approved
'Cause of the Lord
I was not bored.

Caydon Reed (12)

Sport Is For Everyone

From football and tennis to basketball courts,
Everyone can play all kinds of sports.

If you have a disability, that shouldn't hold you back,
Sport is for everyone from pool to track.

If you ever want to be an Olympian, then take your time,
Practice makes perfect to make the finish line.

Imogen Lewis (7)

The Alien Attack

Roses are red, violets are blue,
It's not freezing cold because it's past June,
The time when the fog caved and the snowballs flew,
Has long since passed, just like time,
The heat attacks like a swift ninja at night,
C'mon, take your strike like a player at Wimbledon,
Don't hesitate.

Bencharis Nso (11)

Ben's Life

Once there was a boy called Ben,
He got scouted by Man City at ten.
Ben went on to win and score goals,
Like he had always done.
But one thing happened,
He got an injury to his hamstring.
He retired, then went on to sing.
As life passed, he died,
Because of one very crazy zoo guide.

Dominykas Dapkevicius (10)

Gymnastics

It was a fantastic day.
It was night and the Olympic Games had begun!
Simone Biles is famous for being an athlete.
She has won eight Olympic medals,
And 30 World Championship medals.
Her amazing cartwheels,
She is so flexible and talented.
She is a star and I want to be just like her!

Sahejveer Kaur Sheri (7)

Sports

S port is a great way to keep fit;
P entathlons need one thing: pure grit.
O lympics, or even a small cricket game;
R unning shows stamina; it could lead to fame!
T ennis, taekwondo or even trampoline;
S port climbing and mountaineering for the very keen!

Sahil Agrawal (10)

Swimming With Sharks

I love to swim,
It is my favourite sport.
My dream is to swim with sharks.
I actually had a dream about swimming with sharks,
And it was really amazing!

My favourite place to swim is the sea,
Because after, you can make sandcastles on the beach,
And eat ice cream.

Hailie Valletta (4)

Fantastic Football

F antastic football
O f course, it's fun!
O h, if it was cancelled
T he world would be less fun
B ut we still have it
A lthough some call it lame
L ots of us still love it!
L ose or win, it's an amazing game.

Fatima Ceesay (9)

Swimming

S wim and feel the water carrying you
W ater is soothing
I ntelligent swimming is good in life
M oving freely across the water
M oist, crystal-clear water
I ce-cold water
N ever stop swimming
G lorious cooling water.

Zachary Flounders (9)

Football

F	un with family
O	nly inside when the weather is bad
O	bviously playing lots of football
T	he summertime is the best time
B	eing in the sun
A	ll day, you get a good night's sleep
L	ove the sun
L	ove sports.

Faith Kelly (15)

Paralympic Power

The athletes are like superheroes,
They are super strong and fast,
They don't let anything get them down,
Even if they come last.

Jack is on crutches,
But he's still really good,
When he gets in the pool,
He swims faster than I could!

Jackson Peach (7)

Football

I go to the pitch,
With my friends, Michael, Ben and Mitch.
The ball is round,
As I kick it off the ground.
Skilling attackers,
Leaving their defence knackered.
Straight at the goalkeeper,
I take my shot,
Top bins!

Caden Hamlyn-Harris (11)

A Dream Yet To Be Accomplished

An orange ball high in the air,
Standing on end are my hairs,
Tension leaking from sweat and blood,
It enters the hoop, a roaring flood;
From crowds shrieking, "Joyceee!"
It was just a dream, you silly goose!
A dream yet to be accomplished.

Momin Suleman (13)

Paralympics

P ara-swimming
A rchery
R ugby
A thletics
L ong jump
Y achting
M arathon runners
P owerlifting
I nternational
C losing ceremony
S hooting.

Eilidh Ortega (10)

Running

Running makes me happy, running makes me laugh,
Running makes me want to choose the most exciting path.
The glee that running brings to me, makes me really happy,
I want to be the best I can, so I've got to make it snappy.

Anna Heathcote (7)

Olympics

O is for optimism
L is for legendary
Y is for yearning
M is for motivation
P is for proud
I is for impressive
C is for confident
S is for superstars.

Lilly Wallace (5)

Bryony

B ryony is my gymnastics coach, and she is lovely!
R olls and holds,
Y ou and me, working together,
O n the bar, we spin around,
N ew tricks and flips,
Y ou are a great coach!

Kat McCue (8)

Hockey

H   it the ball with the stick
O   ver the head, you better be quick
C   all your teammate's name
K   eeper better have good aim
E   yes on the ball
Y   ells of "We rule!"

Liv Kennedy (9)

Chess

The pawns go out into the battle first,
And many are struck down,
Then out come the knights,
Rushing past the pawns,
Galloping on,
To the enemy king,
Checkmate by the knight,
That side wins again.

Còiseam Young

Runners

R eady for a breath
U nderdog of the competition
N ever slowing down
N ever tiring
E very race different
R unning their best
S print to the finish.

Ewan Jones (17)

Sportastic

I love gymnastics and football,
I think that they're both really cool,
I like to do them every day,
I do that and also play.
You now shall learn,
Because I know it's your turn.

Amirah Bekhit (9)

Sports, Sports, Sports

Sports, sports, sports,
Don't forget to bring your shorts!
Football, basketball, baseball,
Even ones without a ball.
After school,
Everyone is cool,
Out in the sporting sun!

Jessica Prestage (12)

Gravity Gone - Cloud Ball

Fluffy clouds,
Two pals.
Bing, bong, bang!
Over the cloud wall,
While the boys are in the pool.
Fun game,
But you can't aim.
Bing, bong, bang!

Taylor-Grace Stare (10)

Gymnastics

If you jump off a beam,
Flip off a bar,
You will go far.
You may be frightened or scared,
But there's no need if you are prepared.
Just try your best, you superstar!

Taylor Powell (9)

Mark The Runner

There was a runner,
He always ran in the park,
Even when it was dark.
His name is Mark,
He had a big truck.
One day, he tripped over a rock,
So he ran out of luck.

Zakariya Hersi (9)

Man City

Man City are my team,
When they score,
It makes me scream.
When the other team wins,
I think it's mean,
So to cheer myself up,
I ask my mummy for an ice cream.

Bonnie Taylor (9)

Chess

C   hess is the best
H   opping over pieces with my knight
E   ach time I play, I get better
S   etting up is my favourite part
S   creaming when I win!

Pippa Ward (7)

Sport Is For Me And You

Sport is fabulous,
Basketball and football,
Is nice to play with other people,
But I don't like tackling,
I can play on my own too,
Sport is for me and you.

Miles Lewis (5)

Monopoly

Monopoly: my favourite board game,
Sometimes makes me rack my brain,
But I find out my sum,
And impress everyone,
Though really, it feels just the same!

Elizabeth Byrom (9)

Tennis

A diamanté poem

Racket
Hard, strong
Hits, glides, serves
Smashes powerfully, sails rapidly
Flies, bounces, soars
Round, fast
Tennis ball.

Vaanathi Manikandan (11)

Sport

Summer is the best time for sports,
Keeps you energetic,
Every time,
Never keeps you waiting,
But never do it after dusk!

Thananiya Thevakanthan (9)

Chess

A haiku

Good-room books, time-stop,
Wingback chairs, sound of silence,
Knight takes queen, checkmate!

Brendan Cosgrove (10)

Roller Skating

R ace, glide, spin and jump

O bserving the world as it rapidly rolls by

L eaping from the floor, landing back down so smoothly

L ively and energetic as I skate

E ntertaining crowds whilst I swivel in the air

R oller skating is an exhilarating sport

S ilently, four wheels carry me along

K nocking my wheels against the floor, what a challenge!

A daring sport, as risks are taken to jump high

T he feeling of swirling, my heart loudly beating

I t takes years of practice to be a star, learning prances, swirls, and hops

N ever skip a step; a mistake could be fatal

G old medals, silver medals, and bronze can be won for a flawless performance.

Elsie Honnor (13)

Ansford Academy, Castle Cary

My Forever Home

I am back,
Back to the place where it all began,
Back to the place where I found my first-ever love,
Back to the place I could go to feel free,
Back to the place where I could tumble and flip all my problems away,
After months away, I am back,
Back to the place where I belong,
Where it all started,
My true home,
My forever home.

Lia Chung (13)
Ark Blake Academy, Croydon

Walking Football

Silence everyone,
The game is afoot.
Quick, people - look, look, look!

Watch, they've scored a goal,
They've done it in one fell swoop,
They're holding the trophy.

But wait, what is this?
Goodness me, it's walking on the pitch
It's a foot, that's what.

And look what it's got,
It's kicking a football through,
It waves through the glade.

Then disappears through trees,
It bounces through the ivory field,
Never to be seen.

Eve Antroness
Brixham College, Brixham

Try Your Best

Every second,
Every moment,
Everything,
It all matters.

Mistakes are not an option,
Only perfection,
Your best every time,
It has to be 100% all the time.

The drama,
The excitement,
The motion,
The perseverance.

It all comes down,
Down to that last second,
If you win or lose,
Win or lose?

You were your best,
Though is it the best?
You wait to find out,
Have you won?

Charlie Thomas (15)
Bruern Abbey Senior School, Chilton

Celestial Dance

Upon their canvas of blue and white,
Their airborne stage where they take flight,
What do they use so high in the skies,
To perform their beauty in front of our eyes?

Vibrant silks twirl and entwine,
Crafting patterns ever so divine,
Spinning colours with such daring flair,
The audience can't help but attentively stare.

Twisting through the sapphire sea,
Dancing with what brings them glee,
Drops and climbs ever so bold,
In a tapestry to behold.

Striking hoops of black and blue,
As they lay like a man on the moon,
In their canvas strung up or like a lollipop,
Giving us a show we will remember nonstop.

On their skyline staging ever so clear,
They glow like chandeliers,
And fearless they are when storms arise
With thunder roars and lightning cries.

Soaring through with fearless pace,
No fear of falling, only trust's embrace,

Aerial rope bending the laws of space and time,
A dance that breaks the night's chime.

In the glamour of the sunlight glow,
Suspended where the breezes flow,
Aerial acrobats paint the sky,
In their art, the heavens lie.

Nafisa Chowdhury (13)
Devonport High School For Girls, Peverell

First Place

He started off slow, taunting the other racers
They all ran rapidly towards the finish line.
One by one, the track racers slowed down.

One step. Two steps. Three steps. More.
He had already caught up with track player four.
He was already in second place.
But the person in first place was picking up the pace.

Five steps. Six steps. Seven steps. More.
All the people behind were dropping to the floor.
There was a long way to go
But he couldn't stop
He had gone all this way
So he needed to go faster.

Battling the pain
He finished the race
Everyone is baffled
About how he came in first place.

Karim Rodrick (12)
Friern Barnet School, Friern Barnet

Football

A haiku

The fast, fit players,
The ball went the speed of light,
The players will score.

Omari Bramble

Goddard Park Primary School, Park North

The Olympics

The fast, fit athletes,
Everyone shouts,
"Come on, you can do this!"

Millie May Saunders (9)
Goddard Park Primary School, Park North

The Euros

A haiku

The vibrant green pitch,
The stadium cheered loudly,
They're unstoppable!

Riley Hobbs (9)

Goddard Park Primary School, Park North

Euro 2024

A haiku

The skilful players,
Football is the most tracked sport,
The speedy athletes.

Alfie Pockett (8)

Goddard Park Primary School, Park North

Paralympic Swimming

A haiku

The intense swimming,
Tough Paralympic swimming,
The calm swimming times.

Lola Hamley
Goddard Park Primary School, Park North

Red Bull Stunts

A haiku

Hear the crowd roar now,
The independent builders,
As they fly downtown.

Rayyan Musid (9)

Goddard Park Primary School, Park North

The Olympics

A haiku

The chaotic crowd,
Loudly cheering and roaring,
For the brave athlete.

Genesis Rai (9)

Goddard Park Primary School, Park North

Swimming

A haiku

The huge, intense swim,
The large pool was very loud,
Glorious people.

Christie Do Rosario

Goddard Park Primary School, Park North

The Olympic Games

A haiku

Winning or losing,
Best, worldwide and public games,
People persevere.

Archie Haines (10)

Goddard Park Primary School, Park North

Euro 2024

A haiku

The match was intense,
Everybody was roaring,
Supportive, loud fans.

Jack Saunders (9)
Goddard Park Primary School, Park North

The Olympians

A haiku

Brave Olympians,
The fast, fit athletes compete,
Come on! Persevere!

Faith J (9)

Goddard Park Primary School, Park North

Olympics

A haiku

Hard-working swimmers,
The dark blue water shimmers,
Amazing movers.

Esmai Tina Fanning (9)

Goddard Park Primary School, Park North

The Olympics

A haiku

The hard, intense games,
Terrifying tournaments,
The speedy players.

Alex Lourenco

Goddard Park Primary School, Park North

Tennis

A haiku

He was intensely,
Playing tennis as he fell,
He hit the ball hard.

Alfie W (9)

Goddard Park Primary School, Park North

The Euros

F   eelings of success
O   h, the expectations and tenseness
O   pen to the highs but lows hurt
T   hree lions on the shirt
B   ringing hope and don't forget
A   ction-packed, back of the net
L   osing or winning, the
L   ions will still be singing!

E   ngland's win is dawning
U   nited Kingdom roaring
R   olling ball soaring
O   llie Watkins
S   coring!

Reuben Howe
Running Deer School CIC, Butterdon Wood

E-Games

E   uros brings happiness

-

G   olden goals everywhere
A   stadium full of glee
M   atches eager to start
E   nd of matches barely waiting
S   idelines with refs waiting.

Zayd Rahman (9)
Torridon Primary School, Catford

The Olympic Games

I am going to the Olympic Games
I will help my team win
Each athlete has aims
When we win, we will show a grin

We have a lot of confidence
We will be happy when we get the trophy
The athletes must run a certain distance
The athletes will enjoy coffee after their win
I will scream in joy when our team wins
Their kids will bring toys
The kids will have honorary fins
The kids will make a screaming noise

When we get the trophy, I will scream
The athletes will bring the trophy home
The athletes will have steam coming off their legs
The athletes can speak into the microphone

The athletes can take the trophy to their country
This is the big time of the year
The athletes will be hungry after the Olympics
They will go faster than Santa's reindeer.

Archer Findlay (9)
Unity Academy, Blackpool

The Olympics

O lympics is intense to watch

L eg races, swimming, you name it

Y ou can do all sorts of sports

M aybe you might become Olympic champion one day

P icture yourself winning the Olympics and everyone cheering for you

I n the Olympics, you can show off the best you've ever been

C hildren and adults will watch as it goes worldwide

S o that proves that the Olympics is a fun thing to do and watch!

Molly Elliott (10)

Unity Academy, Blackpool

The Olympic History

Haiku poetry

The Olympic rings,
They symbolise the great Games,
They are coloured rings.

Olympics were held,
In honour of the Greek god,
The almighty Zeus!

Amazing Usain,
The fastest man in the world,
Has eight world records!

But who has the most?
The great swimmer, Michael Phelps!
With big 28.

They have history,
They have lots of sport and sweat,
The Olympics rule!

Poppy Mellor (10)
Unity Academy, Blackpool

Talking Part In The Olympic Games

It looks familiar,
I am going insane,
I hope I get that much fame.

I won the race - I got a gold medal,
Shining bright like a precious metal,
Time to do swimming.

I am a slow swimmer but I got third place,
Another medal - hip, hip, hooray!
One of my colleagues used spray.

Lyla Leech (10)
Unity Academy, Blackpool

The Olympics Are Back

O lympics are back
L ots of people
Y ou're all watching
M edals are getting handed out
P eople everywhere
I am going to win
C oach giving advice
S omeday, I am getting the gold.

Sophia Jade Jeffries (10)
Unity Academy, Blackpool

The Olympics

O lympics are here
L ots of fun
Y ellow is everywhere
M edals are on the podium
P eople are everywhere
I am on the podium
C oach is nice
S omeday, I will get the gold medal!

Emily Houghton (10)
Unity Academy, Blackpool

Taking Part

Haiku poetry

On the pitch today,
And all the countries chanting,
I was feeling scared.

As scared as I was,
I also felt excited,
It felt amazing.

I scored the first goal,
The feeling was fantastic,
Everyone chanted.

Reece Whetton (10)

Unity Academy, Blackpool

YoungWriters Est. 1991

YOUNG WRITERS

We hope you have enjoyed reading this book – and that you will continue to in the coming years.

If you're the parent or family member of an enthusiastic poet or story writer, do visit our website **www.youngwriters.co.uk/subscribe** and sign up to receive news, competitions, writing challenges and tips, activities and much, much more! There's lots to keep budding writers motivated!

If you would like to order further copies of this book, or any of our other titles, then please give us a call or order via your online account.

Young Writers
Remus House
Coltsfoot Drive
Peterborough
PE2 9BF
(01733) 890066
info@youngwriters.co.uk

Join in the conversation!
Tips, news, giveaways and much more!

f YoungWritersUK   **X** YoungWritersCW

📷 youngwriterscw   **♪** youngwriterscw